High Density Data Centers

Case Studies and Best Practices

This publication was prepared in cooperation with TC 9.9, Mission Critical Facilities, Technology Spaces, and Electronic Equipment.

High Density Data Centers

American Society of Heating, Refrigerating and Air-Conditioning Engineers, Inc.

ISBN 978-1-933742-32-8

Second imprint ©2008 American Society of Heating, Refrigerating
and Air-Conditioning Engineers, Inc.
1791 Tullie Circle, NE
Atlanta, GA 30329
www.ashrae.org

Cover courtesy of Joe Lombardo of DLB Associates.

Library of Congress Cataloging-in-Publication Data

High density data centers : case studies and best practices.
    p. cm. — (ASHRAE Datacom Series)
  Summary: "Provides the reader a series of data center case studies and best practices that demonstrate how high density loads can be cooled using a number of different approaches and includes a breadth of data center ventilation schemes and shows how they are deployed to cool high density IT equipment"—Provided by publisher.
  Includes bibliographical references and index.
  ISBN 978-1-933742-32-8 (softcover)
  1. Office buildings--Design and construction--Case studies. 2. Office buildings--Air conditioning--Case studies. 3. Electronic data processing departments--Equipment and supplies--Protection--Case studies. 4. Data processing service centers--Equipment and supplies--Protection--Case studies. 5. Electronic digital computers--Cooling--Case studies. 6. Data libraries--Protection--Case studies. I. American Society of Heating, Refrigerating and Air-Conditioning Engineers.

TH4311.H54 2008
725'.23--dc22

                        2008006301

ASHRAE STAFF

Contents

Acknowledgments

The information in this book was produced with the help and support of the corporations, academic institutions, and organizations listed below:

American Power Conversion	JDA Consulting Engineers
Bellsouth	Lawrence Berkeley National Lab
Cedar Sinai Medical Center	Microsoft
Citigroup	Minick Engineering
Cushman and Wakefield	Opengate Data Systems
DLB Associates Consulting Engineers	Oracle
Emerson	Panduit
Georgia Institute of Technology	Rumsey Engineers
Hewlett Packard	San Diego Supercomputer Center
IBM	Ted Jacob Engineering Group

ASHRAE TC9.9 wants to particularly thank the following people:

- **John Bean**, **Christian Belady**, **Jack Glass**, **Jason Kutticherry**, **Oleg Levchook**, **Rhonda Johnson**, **Bret Lehman**, **Mukesh Khattar**, **Joe Prisco**, **Madhusudan Iyengar**, and **Roger Schmidt** for their participation as chapter leads and for writing and performing final edits of their chapters.
- **Dr. Roger Schmidt** of IBM, Chair of TC9.9, for his vision and leadership in the creation of this book.
- **Joe Lombardo** for the book cover design.

In addition TC9.9 would like to thank Will Dahlmeier, Mike Mangan, and Don Beaty of DLB Associates, Inc., and the following people for substantial contributions to the individual case studies in the book:

Case 1: Thanks to Bob Wasilewski and Tom Juliano of DLB Associates, Inc. for aiding in the measurements, and thanks to Donna Upright and Duane Oetjen of IBM for their complete support in performing these measurements while the data center was in full operation.

Case 2: Thanks to Bob Wasilewski and Tom Juliano of DLB Associates, Inc., for their aid in the measurements, and thanks to Donna Upright and Duane Oetjen for their complete support in performing these measurements while the data center was in full operation.

Case 3: Thanks to Dr. Roger Schmidt, Dr. Hendrik Hamann, Dane Miller, and Harald Zettl for their help with collection and interpretation of the data. The characterization and paper would not have been possible without their contribution. The author also thanks the staff of SDSC, especially Mike Datte and Jeff Filliez, for their full cooperation in allowing IBM to study the data center and publish the results.

Case 4: Thanks to Donna Upright and Duane Oetjen for their complete support in performing these measurements in Poughkeepsie while the data center was in full operation.

Case 5: Thanks to Steve Holt at Livermore for helping with the data collection at the Livermore site.

Case 6: Thanks to Gerhard Haub and Patrick Calcagno of Cushman and Wakefield and Ryan Meadows and Ed Koplin of JDA Consulting Engineers for their assistance with field measurements and analysis.

Case 7: Thanks to Dr. Bartosz Ilkowski at the Georgia Institute of Technology, Bret Lehman of IBM, Stephen Peet of BellSouth, and Steve Battenfeld of Minick Engineering for their contributions to both the design and documentation of this high density case study. Thanks also to Sam Toas and Rhonda Johnson of Panduit for their contributions in the areas of temperature measurement and results documentation.

Case 8: Thanks to Jonathan Lomas for field data collection and Scott Buell for CFD modeling and graphics.

Case 9: Thanks to Lennart Stahl of Emerson, a great collaborator on the project, and to the supporting executives, Paul Perez of HP and Thomas Bjarnemark of Emerson. Thanks also to Chandrakant Patel, Cullen Bash, and Roy Zeighami for all their technical support and contributions.

Case 10: Thanks to Dr. Mukesh Khattar, Mitch Martin, Stephen Metcalf, and Keith Ward of Oracle for conceptual design and implementation of the hot-air containment at the rack level, which permitted use of variable-speed drives on the CRACs while preventing mixing of hot and cold air in the data floor; Mark Redmond of Ted Jacob Engineering Group for system engineering and specifications; and Mark Germagian, formerly of Wright Line and now with Opengate Data Systems, for building server racks with hot-air containment.

Case 11: Thanks to Bill Tschudi of Lawrence Berkeley National Laboratory and Peter Rumsey of Rumsey Engineers for contributing this case study, which was performed as part of a broader project for the California Energy Commission.

1

Introduction

Data centers and telecommunications rooms that house datacom equipment are becoming increasingly more difficult to adequately cool. This is a result of IT manufacturers increasing datacom performance year after year at the cost of increased heat dissipation. Even though performance has, in general, increased at a more rapid rate than power, the power required and the resulting heat dissipated by the datacom equipment has increased to a level that is putting a strain on data centers. However, in the struggle to improve the thermal management characteristics of data centers it is sometimes important to assess today's data center designs. The objective of this book is to provide a series of case studies of high density data centers and a range of ventilation schemes that demonstrate how loads can be cooled using a number of different approaches.

This introductory chapter describes the various ventilation designs most often employed within data centers. This book does not present an exhaustive resource for existing ventilation schemes but, rather, a wide variety of schemes commonly used in the industry. Seven primary ventilation schemes are outlined here. In the case studies that follow, each of these will be shown with detailed measurements of airflow, power, and temperature.

The most common ventilation design for data centers is the raised-access floor supply, with racks arranged in a cold-aisle/hot-aisle layout (see Figure 1.1). The chilled-air supply enters the room through perforated tiles in the raised floor, washing the fronts of the racks facing the cold aisle. The hot exhaust air from the racks then migrates back to the inlet of the computer room air-conditioning units (CRACs) typically located on the perimeter of the data center.

Another version of the raised-access floor supply is shown in Figure 1.2, where the air-handling units (AHUs) are located beneath the floor containing the IT equipment. One of the key advantages of this arrangement is that all the mechanical equipment is located in a room separate from the IT equipment, which allows for ease of maintenance.

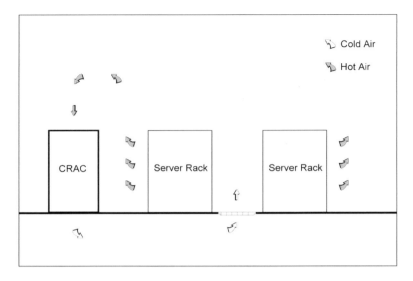

Figure 1.1 Raised-access floor supply.

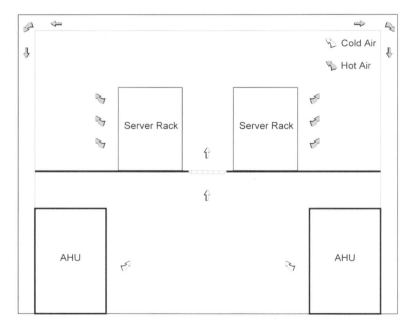

Figure 1.2 Raised-access floor with air-handling unit on floor below.

A slightly different version of the raised-access floor supply is the raised-access floor supply and ceiling return, as shown in Figure 1.3. This is an advantageous design for high-powered racks with hot exhaust, since the hot air is pulled from the hot aisle before it is allowed to mix with the cold air. The higher return air temperature allows the CRACs to operate much more efficiently given the higher return air temperature.

A unique layout for raised-access floors is shown in Figure 1.4. In this case, the modular CRACs are laid out in the data center in the hot aisle. The advantage of this ventilation scheme is that the hot-air exhaust from the racks has a short path to the inlet of the CRACs, and the chilled air exhausting from the CRACs has a short path to the cold-aisle perforated tiles. Both paths are short, thereby minimizing the impedance to airflow. The heat load capability of the CRACs needs to be somewhat balanced with the heat load of the racks in the immediate vicinity.

Since the heat load of the racks has become quite high, there are several options now offered in the industry that provide localized air-to-liquid heat exchangers. In these cases, the localized air-to-liquid heat exchanger, as shown in Figure 1.5, removes most—if not all—of the heat load from the rack before it exhausts into the larger data center room. This removes any hot-spot potential in the room.

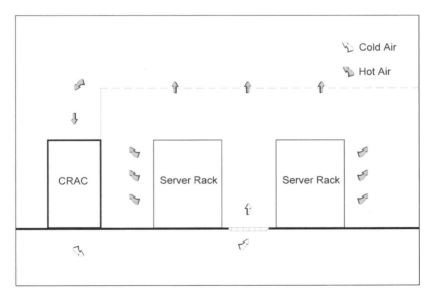

Figure 1.3 Raised-access floor supply/ceiling return.

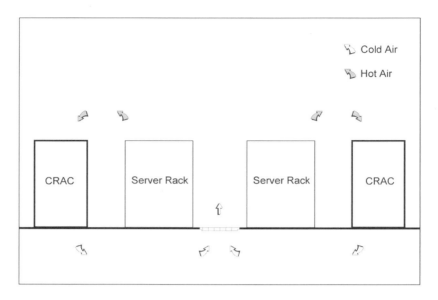

Figure 1.4   Raised floor with modular CRACs in hot aisle.

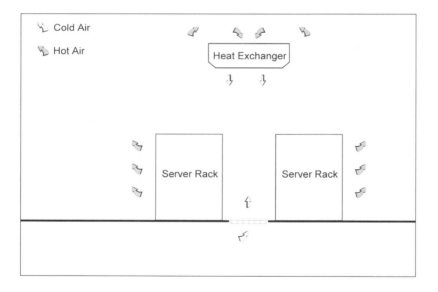

Figure 1.5   Raised-access floor with air-to-liquid heat exchangers adjacent to IT racks.

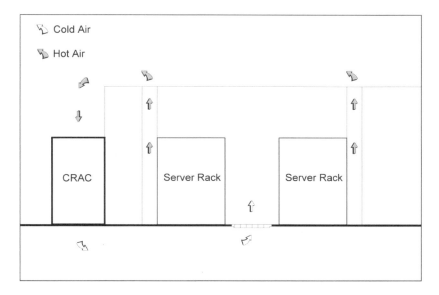

Figure 1.6 Raised-access floor supply/ducted ceiling return.

To further separate the hot exhaust air from the racks and the cold air in the cold aisle, Figure 1.6 shows a ducted hot-air exhaust back to the CRACs. The ducting is an effective separation technique but needs to be closely integrated with the IT racks.

Figure 1.7 shows a non-raised-access floor design in which supply chilled air enters from the ceiling, and hot-air exhaust from the racks returns to the CRACs located on the perimeter of the data center.

The following chapters provide case studies of operational data centers with the ventilation schemes described above. The purpose of these studies is to be as complete as possible in deploying measured thermal parameters of the data center. For most cases, these include inlet air temperatures to each rack; airflow rates from perforated tiles and other openings, such as cable openings; power measurements of all elements within the data center, including IT equipment, lighting, and power distribution units (PDUs); and, finally, a complete set of geometric parameters that describe the data center, including rack layouts, raised-access floor heights (if a floor is raised), ceiling heights, and any other information pertinent to the thermal management of the data center. Although thermal modeling is not the subject of this book, one could theoretically use the data from these case studies to construct a thermal model of the data center and then make comparisons.

The format for displaying the data is the same for most of the case studies so that comparisons can be made between the various ventilation schemes as desired.

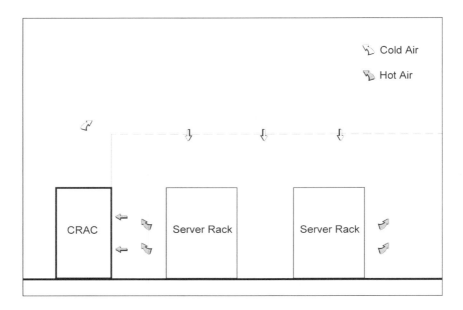

Figure 1.7   Non-raised-access floor ceiling supply.

The two chapters devoted to case studies cover raised-access floors and non-raised-access floors. Since most measurements are for raised floors, several subcategories are provided in which case studies are shown for each subcategory. Chapter 4 is devoted to best practices for each of the primary categories of ventilation schemes—raised-access and non-raised-access floors. These guidelines are based on technical papers published mostly within the last five years, and also from the case studies presented herein.

Chapter 5 provides an expanded list of references and a bibliography with additional, related materials. Chapter 6 provides a useful glossary of common terms used throughout this book.

2

Raised-Access Floor
Case Studies

2.1   RAISED-ACCESS FLOOR WITH PERIMETER MODULAR CRACs

2.1.1   CASE STUDY 1—NATIONAL CENTER
FOR ENVIRONMENTAL PREDICTION (NCEP)

The heat dissipated by large servers and switching equipment has reached levels that make it very difficult to cool these systems. Some of the highest-powered systems dissipate up to 4000 W/ft^2 (43,600 W/m^2) based on the equipment footprint. Systems that dissipate this amount of heat and are clustered together within a data center present significant cooling challenges. This case study describes the thermal profile of a 74 × 84 ft (22.4 × 25.4 m) data center and the measurement techniques employed to fully capture the detailed thermal environment. In a portion of the data center (48 × 56 ft [14.5 × 17.0 m]) that encompasses the servers, the heat flux is 170 W/ft^2 (1850 W/m^2). Most racks within this area dissipated 6.8 kW, while a couple dissipated upward of 28 kW. Detailed measurements were taken of electronic equipment power usage, perforated floor tile airflow, cable cut-out airflow, CRAC airflow, temperatures and power usage, and electronic equipment inlet air temperatures. In addition to these measurements, the physical features of the data center were recorded.

LAYOUT OF DATA CENTER

The National Center for Environmental Prediction (NCEP) data center is located in Bethesda, Maryland. All of the equipment is positioned on a raised-access floor in an enclosed area that is 74 × 84 ft (22.4 × 25.4 m). A plan view of the data center indicating the location of the electronic equipment PDUs, CRACs, and perforated floor tiles is shown in Figure 2.1. Most of the servers (51 racks) are IBM model 7040 (p690). The other systems are a mix of switching, communication, and storage equipment. The key classes of equipment are highlighted in Figure 2.1. The ceiling height, as measured from the raised-access floor to the ceiling, is 10 ft (3.03 m) with

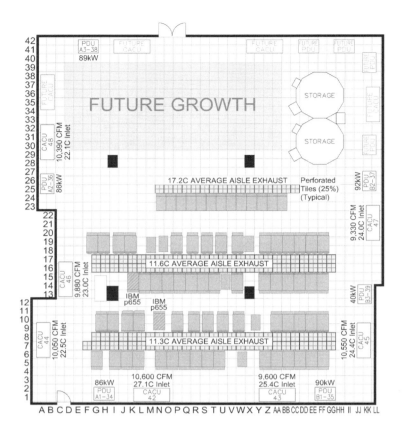

Figure 2.1 NCEP datacom equipment layout.

a raised-access floor height of 17 in. (431.8 mm). Seven operational CRACs and six operational PDUs are located around the perimeter of the room. Potential expansion is anticipated, and additional PDUs and CRACs (shown as "Future") are shown in Figure 2.1. The servers are located in a cold-aisle/hot-aisle arrangement with aisle widths of approximately 4 ft (1.2 m [two floor tiles]). The cold aisles were populated with 25% open tiles with dampers removed on all the tiles. A cold aisle showing the rows of racks is displayed in Figure 2.2. In addition, underfloor blockages occurred beneath the raised-access floor. These were either insulated chilled-water pipes, as shown in Figure 2.3, or cabling located beneath the server equipment.

When the data center was first populated with equipment, high rack inlet air temperatures were measured at a number of rack locations. The problem was that the perimeter between the raised-access floor and subfloor was not blocked off, and the

Figure 2.2   Cold aisle showing racks.

Figure 2.3   Blockages underneath the raised-access floor.

chilled air from the CRACs was exiting to other portions of the building (this data center was centrally located among other raised-access floor data and office spaces). In addition, the total heat dissipation of the electronic equipment in the room exceeded the sensible cooling capacity of the CRAC. Based on these problems, an additional CRAC was installed, and the entire perimeter of the region between the raised-access floor and subfloor was enclosed. (Although before-and-after results will not be presented in this paper, the resulting flow increased by about 50%, and the rack inlet temperatures decreased on average by about 5°C (41°F) with these two changes.)

MEASUREMENT TOOLS

The airflow through the perforated floor tiles, cable cut-outs, and CRACs was measured with a velometer. The unit was calibrated on a wind tunnel, and all measurements were adjusted based on the calibration (the velometer measured approximately 4% low for the range of airflows measured).

The temperatures were measured with a high-accuracy handheld digital thermometer using a type T thermocouple. Since temperature differences and not absolute temperatures were of most importance, the meter was not calibrated. Temperature difference errors were estimated to be ±1.0°C (±1.8°F), resulting primarily from cycling of the CRACs.

Voltage and current measurements of the CRACs were made with a handheld voltmeter and a current clamp-on meter. Manufacturer data reported the error in these devices as ±0.7% and ±2%, respectively.

The input power of several racks was measured by connecting a laptop with custom software to the server.

MEASUREMENT METHODOLOGY AND RESULTS

Power Measurements

Measurements of input power to the data center were made at several levels in order to provide a good estimate of the input power of various types of equipment. The overall data center input power was taken from the PDUs located around the perimeter of room (see Figure 2.1). These provided input power only to the electronic equipment within the room, not including the CRACs or lighting. Each PDU provided input power in kW, the results of which are shown in Table 2.1. The total input power of all the data processing equipment was 483 kW. All electronic racks operated with a power factor correction of nearly 1.0 with three-phase 208 V input to the racks.

The CRACs and lighting also contribute to the overall heat load in the data center. Power dissipation of each CRAC was estimated based on voltage and current measurements, as shown in Table 2.1. (Since alternating current motors operate the blowers, a power factor of 0.9 was assumed in estimating the total power dissipated.) Of course, some of the energy put into the CRACs is devoted to fan power. With a pressure drop of approximately 1.2 in. (30.5 mm) of water across the coil and an average airflow rate of 10,060 cfm (279.2 m³/min) (see the "Airflow Measurements" section below), the estimated fan power was approximately 1400 W per CRAC. Lighting was provided by fluorescent fixtures rated at 64 W each. With 78 fixtures in the data center, the resulting total lighting heat load was 5000 W. Therefore, the total heat load in the data center was 520 kW. The maximum error in this total heat load value is estimated to be ±2%.

The more difficult determination was the distribution of power among the individual racks. Given the time constraints (six hours to do all measurements), power

Table 2.1　Power Distribution, kW

Equipment	Power, kW
CRACs	
CACU-47	5.6
CACU-45	6.8
CACU-43	6.7
CACU-42	6.3
CACU-44	6.9
CACU-46	6.6
CACU-48	7.5
Subtotal CRAC Power	**46.4**
Subtotal Lights (78 fixtures)	**5**
PDUs	
B2-37	92
B3-39	40
B1-35	90
A1-34	86
A2-36	86
A3-38	89
Subtotal PDU Power to Electronics	**483**
Total Power Dissipated in Data Center	**534.4**
Breakdown of PDU Power to Electronics	
FasT500 (6)	31
STK (2)	15
HPSS (2)	9
Hans	2
p655 (2)	52
Other (14)	28
p690 (51)	347
Total Electronic Rack Power (R21–R27)	**483**

usage of each rack could not be measured. The focus of the measurements was thus placed on key components crucial to determine the distribution of power in the data center. The majority of the servers (51 racks of IBM model p690) were essentially the same and dissipated similar heat; therefore, measuring a couple of these systems was deemed acceptable. Also, there were two fully configured IBM model p655 racks that dissipated a very high heat load. Given that there were only two of these systems, they were both scheduled for measurement. However, since communications could not be established with these racks, the same rack configurations in another lab were measured. The results for the p690s were 7.2 and 6.6 kW, while two p655s were 26.4 and 27.3 kW. These power measurements were made by a power tool connected directly to the racks. The breakdown of the data-processing rack input powers is shown in Table 2.1. For rack input powers that were not measured, estimates were obtained from the power profile of each. The rack input powers are displayed as a bar graph in Figures 2.4–2.8, with each rack power bar somewhat in line with the physical location of the racks shown in the picture at the top of the figure.

Airflow Measurements

The airflow from the perforated floor tiles was measured with a velometer. This flow tool fit exactly over one perforated tile, so it provided an excellent tool for rapidly profiling the flow throughout the data center. Measured flows from each tile or cable cut-out were very stable, varying <10 cfm (0.28 m^3/min). The measured flow rates from each perforated tile are shown in Figures 2.4–2.8. As in the display of the rack powers, the airflows from the perforated tiles and cable cut-outs are aligned with the physical layout of the perforated tiles and cable cut-outs shown in the picture at the top of the figure.

Measuring the cable cut-out airflows could not be achieved directly since it would have been impossible to locate the flow tool directly over the cable cut-out, which is within the footprint of the rack at the rear. However, an alternative method was proposed and verified to obtain an estimate of the airflow through a cable cut-out (or other openings throughout the data center, such as within the PDU footprint, etc.). First, a cable cut-out was completely blocked with foam materials. Next, a tile with a cut-out of the shape of the cable was provided and placed in the opening nearest the cable opening. To mimic the blockage contributed by the cables, a piece of tape was used to block a portion of the simulated cut-out. The flow through the simulated tile was then measured with the flow tool. Then the blockage was removed from the cable cut-out and the airflow through the simulated tile was repeated. Comparison of these flows, with and without blockage of the cable cut-out, showed no discernible difference in the flow rates measured. Therefore, all cable cut-outs were measured with this modified tile without blocking the actual cable cut-out, which saved a significant amount of time. Some cut-outs were a different size, so the simulated tile was adjusted to approximate the actual opening. The airflow measurements from the cable cut-outs are also shown in Figures 2.4–2.8. Similar to the rack power results, the airflows from the cable and PDU openings are somewhat aligned with the physical layout shown at the top of each figure.

The overall airflow of the data center was estimated based on all the measurements of airflow from the perforated floor tiles and cable cut-outs. The sum of all these measurements was 67,167 cfm (1864.7 m^3/min), after adjusting for the calibration in the flowmeter. Again, the perimeter of the data center below the raised-access floor was completely enclosed such that negligible air escaped the room. One

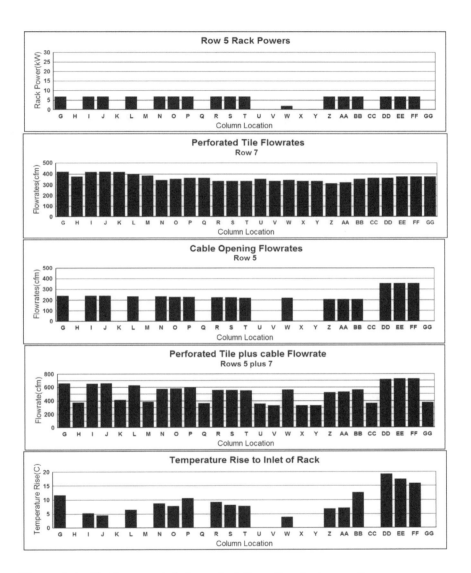

Figure 2.4 Environmental characteristics of racks in row 5.

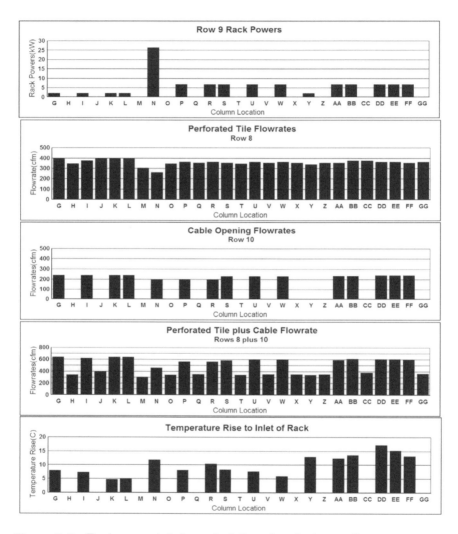

Figure 2.5 Environmental characteristics of racks in row 9.

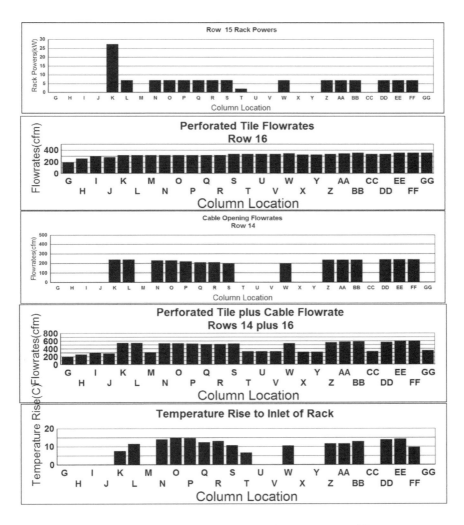

Figure 2.6 Environmental characteristics of racks in row 15.

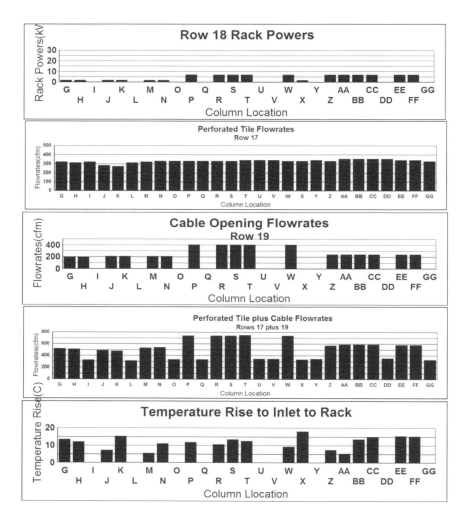

Figure 2.7 Environmental characteristics of racks in row 18.

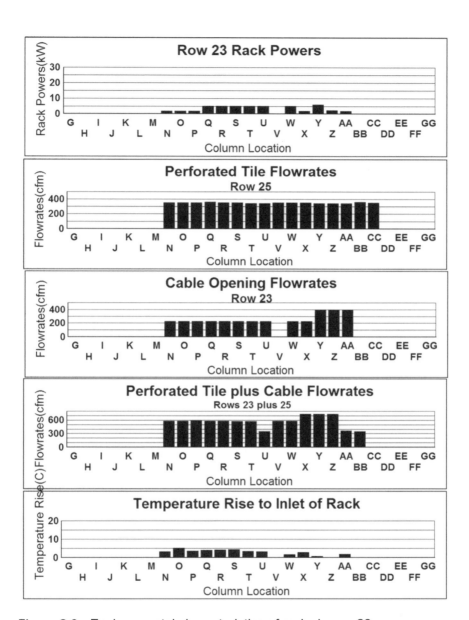

Figure 2.8 Environmental characteristics of racks in row 23.

additional area of airflow not accounted for was the leakage of air that occurred between the perforated tiles. Tate Access (2004) states that a typical air leakage is 0.69 cfm/ft^2 (0.21 m^3/min/m^2) at a static pressure of 0.05 in. (1.27 mm) of water. Since modeling of the flow beneath the floor showed underfloor static pressures of approximately 0.03 in. (0.76 mm) of water, the air leakage was estimated to be 0.50 cfm/ft^2 (0.15 m^3/min/m^2). As the data center had an area of 6200 ft^2 (568.5 m^2), the total air leakage was estimated to be 3200 cfm (88.9 m^3/min). This resulted in a total estimated data center airflow rate of 70,400 cfm (1955 m^3/min). No leakage occurred at the walls around the perimeter of the data center since the side walls rested on top of the raised-access floor and not on the subfloor. The error in the total data center flow rate was estimated to be 4.5% (10% for cable cut-outs and 4% for perforated floor tiles).

The final airflow measurement focused on the flow through each CRAC. These flows are difficult to measure, as there is no easy way to obtain the airflow exhausting the CRACs beneath the floor since it is nonuniform and highly turbulent. Nor is it easy to obtain the total flow entering the CRAC at its inlet. The estimated flow from the CRACs is 10,060 cfm (279.3 m^3/min) (70,400 cfm per seven CRACs or 279.3 m^3/min per CRAC). However, each CRAC displayed some differences in flow due to backpressures under the floor, varying filter cleanliness, variations in the unit, etc., so the velometer was employed to obtain an estimate of the variation in airflow between the units. Basically, a grid of flow measurements was taken across the face of the CRAC and used to tabulate the average velocity. From the average velocity and area, the total airflow into the CRAC was computed. First, the velometer was placed above the CRAC at the inlet to measure a portion of the flow entering the unit. Obviously the flow is not the same, since the opening into the top of the tool (14 × 14 in.) (355.6 × 355.6 mm) is not the same as the opening in the bottom (23 × 23 in.) (584.2 × 584.2 mm). Therefore, the measured airflow will be less than the actual airflow. Measurements at six locations were averaged and multiplied by the area of the inlet of the CRAC, and the measured flow was about two-thirds of the actual flow (computational fluid dynamics [CFD] modeling of the tool at the inlet proved this to be correct). These measurements were then used to proportion the flow among CRACs, the estimates of which are shown in Figure 2.1.

These CRAC airflows do not agree with what is provided by the manufacturer in their catalog for this model unit (12,400 cfm, as stated in the manufacturer's catalog). There are two possible reasons for this. First, each CRAC had a turning vane and side baffle to direct airflow beneath the raised-access floor and, second, each CRAC had slightly dirty filters. So the reduced flow rate of 19%, compared to the catalog value, is not unreasonable.

Temperature Measurements

Temperatures were measured for the supply air flowing from the perforated floor tiles, the air inlet into the racks at a height of 68.9 in. (1750 mm), and the return air to the CRACs. The temperature differences between the raised-access floor supply air temperature and the temperature of the air entering the rack at a height of 68.9 in. (1750 mm) is shown in Figures 2.4–2.8. Temperatures were taken in accordance with ASHRAE (2004) guidelines—2 in. (50 mm) in front of the covers. The graph of the rise in inlet air temperatures (air temperature at a height of 68.9 in. [1750 mm] minus temperature exhaust from the perforated tiles) for each rack is shown at the bottom of each figure. The temperature bars in the graphs are somewhat in line with the rack positions shown at the top of the figure. This provides the reader an interpretation of the spatial temperature distribution, given the flow distribution and the physical layout of the equipment. Return air temperatures at each CRAC were also measured (see Figure 2.1).

ANALYSIS AND COMPARISONS

Thermal Profiles

Several correlations between airflow and air temperature rise at the racks were attempted. None seemed to show any promise; however, several observations can be made. First, airflow through the cable cut-outs is significant—approximately one-third of the total flow is from the cable cut-outs and other openings on the floor. Although the flow from the cable cut-outs can provide some cooling, the analysis by Schmidt and Cruz (2002a) shows this is not the best use of the supply air from the raised-access floor. If the hot exhaust air exiting the racks is drawn back into the inlet of the rack, then the chilled air exhausting the cable cut-outs cools this exhaust air before it enters into the front of the racks. Second, the rack inlet air temperatures for the racks in rows 5 and 9 and located at columns DD, EE, and FF in Figures 2.4–2.8 show relative high temperatures. This may be due to air from the hot aisles returning to the nearby CACU-43 and 45 units and causing the racks to draw in some of this return exhaust air from the racks.

The supply air from the perforated floor tiles adjacent to the IBM p690 racks, along with the corresponding temperature rise to the inlet of the racks, is depicted in Figure 2.9. The average airflow rate from perforated tiles adjacent to the p690 racks is 342 cfm (9.68 m^3/min). The average temperature rise to the inlet of the racks at a height of 68.9 in. (1750 mm) from the raised-access floor is 18.9°F (10.5°C). In addition, the average airflow rate from the cable cut-outs for the p690s is 210 cfm (5.94 m^3/min). Finally, the chilled airflow rates stated here should be compared to the airflow rate through the rack, which is approximately 1100 cfm (31.1 m^3/min). Since each rack extends in width 1.25 tiles, one can assume the total flow to the face of a rack is an average of 427 cfm (12.09 m^3/min) (1.25 × 342 cfm or 1.25 × 9.7 m^3/min). Adding this flow to the cable cut-out flow of 210 cfm (5.94 m^3/min), the total chilled airflow devoted to one rack is approximately 637 cfm (18.0 m^3/min). It is obvious that the airflow rate from the floor in the region of the rack is much less than the flow rate through the rack; however, the air inlet temperatures to the racks are still well within the rack temperature specs (50°F–89.6°F [10°C–32°C]). If the cable cut-out and

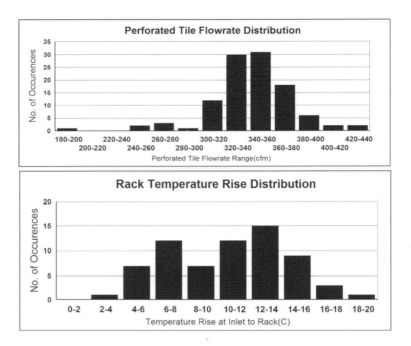

Figure 2.9   Flow rate and temperature distribution in region of p690s.

perforated tile adjacent to the rack were combined to provide the chilled airflow to the rack, then the temperature rise with this flow and a rack heat load of 6.8 kW would be 34.2°F (19°C). Since the temperature rise to the top of the rack averages 18.9°F (10.5°C), the temperature plume exhausting the rear of the racks must mix with the air in a larger region, thereby damping the temperature rise. This suggests there is enough mixing in the room to bring the exhaust temperatures down, even though the local chilled airflow rates are much lower than what might be considered adequate.

Energy Balance

To confirm the accuracy of the data via an energy balance, a calculation of airflow using measured power input and temperature difference was compared to the actual measured airflow to see if they matched. The overall data center airflow, as measured from the perforated floor tiles and other openings, was 70,400 cfm (1993 m³/min), with an estimated accuracy of 4.5%. Also, the error in the temperature difference of 22.4°F (12.45°C), as measured at the underfloor and the return to the CRACs, was estimated to be 10%. Finally, the error of 534.4 kW in the overall heat dissipation in the data center was estimated to be 2%. Using the CRAC average temperature difference and the overall heat load for the data center (534.4 kW), the expected data center flow rate is 77,262 cfm (2187 m^3/min) ±10.2% (69,381–85,142 cfm [1964–2410 m^3/min]). This calculation compares favorably to the measured value of 70,400 cfm (1993 m^3/min) ±4.5% (67,230–73,570 cfm [1903–2083 m^3/min]). From this examination of measured data center flow rate compared to calculated flow rate based on an energy balance, measurements are found to be within reason, and closure on the energy balance is obtained.

SUMMARY

A methodology was outlined and described with the aid of measurements collected from a high density data center. The components of the measurements include the following:

- Power
  - ✓ PDU
  - ✓ Racks
  - ✓ Lighting
  - ✓ CRAC

- Temperatures
  - ✓ Rack inlet air
  - ✓ CRAC return air
  - ✓ Supply air from perforated floor tiles

- Airflows
  - ✓ CRAC
  - ✓ Perforated floor tiles
  - ✓ Cable cut-outs
  - ✓ PDU openings

These measurements allowed for a detailed thermal profile of the data center.

The airflow through the perforated tiles was approximately one-quarter to one-half of the airflow through the rack, in order to maintain system inlet air temperatures in accordance with the specifications. The perforated tile airflow rate plus the cable cut-out flow rate was about one-half to two-thirds of the airflow through the rack. Even though the room flow rate was adequate to cool the overall heat load in the data center, and the local flow rate adjacent to the racks did not appear adequate, the convection currents that occurred at room level were adequate to bring local air temperatures for the high-powered racks within the temperature specifications.

Airflows through the CRACs were quite low compared to published values from the manufacturer. The average airflow through a CRAC was 10,400 cfm (294.5 m^3/min) compared to the manufacturer's catalog value of 12,400 cfm (351.1 m^3/min), a 19% reduction. Although unverified, it is the authors' opinion that this reduction was a result of turning vanes and side baffles installed on the CRAC units.

This case study describes a specific set of measurements from a high density data center in order to provide details of the thermal profile. In addition, the data collection techniques described can be used as a basis for collecting data from other data centers or telecom rooms and provide a presentation format in which to display the information.

REFERENCES

ASHRAE. 2004. *Thermal Guidelines for Data Processing Environments*. Atlanta: American Society of Heating, Refrigerating and Air-Conditioning Engineers, Inc.

Schmidt, R., and E. Cruz. 2002a. Raised floor computer data center: Effect on rack inlet temperatures of exiting both the hot and cold aisle. *Proceedings of Itherm Conference 2002, San Diego, CA,* pp. 580–94.

Tate Access Floors. 2004. Controlling air leakage from raised access floor cavities. Technical Bulletin #216, Tate Access Floors, Inc., Jessup, MD.

2.1.2 CASE STUDY 2— IBM TEST FACILITY IN POUGHKEEPSIE (2004)

This section describes the thermal profile of a 76 × 98 ft (23.2 × 29.9 m) data center and the measurement techniques employed to fully capture the detailed thermal environment. In a portion of the data center (16 × 26 ft [4.9 × 7.9 m]) that encompasses very high-powered servers, the heat flux was512 W/ft^2 (5500 W/m^2). Most racks within this area dissipated approximately 19 kW. Detailed measurements were taken of electronic equipment power usage, perforated floor tile airflow, cable cutout airflow, CRAC airflow, and electronic equipment inlet air temperatures. In addition to these measurements, the physical features of the data center were recorded such that a detailed CFD model could be employed to compare the results (not described herein).

LAYOUT OF DATA CENTER

The IBM development lab is located in Poughkeepsie, NY. The data center is used to configure and test large clusters of systems before shipping to a customer. From time to time, test clusters afford an opportunity for measurements. The systems in this data center are located on a raised-access floor in an area 76 × 98 ft (23.2 × 29.9 m). A plan view of the data center indicating the location of the electronic equipment, CRACs, and perforated floor tiles is shown in Figure 2.10.

The area is part of a larger data center not shown in the figure. In order to thermally isolate this area from other parts of the data center for the purposes of this study, several temporary partitions were installed. Plastic sheets were draped from the ceiling tiles to the floor along row 49, shown in Figure 2.10. This concentrated the heat load from the systems to the CRACs located in the area of interest. To further separate the area, the underfloor plenum was examined for openings around the perimeter of the portion of the room. Openings underneath the floor (cable and pipe openings, etc.) were also closed off. The above-floor and below-floor blockages are shown in Figure 2.11.

Two primary server racks populated this data center: the IBM model 7040 (p690) accounted for 79 systems and the IBM model 7039 (p655) accounted for 23 systems. The other systems were a mix of switching, communication, and storage equipment. The key classes of equipment are highlighted in Figure 2.12. The ceiling height, as measured from the raised-access floor to the ceiling, was 108 in. (2.74 m), with a raised-access floor height of 28 in. (0.7 m). Twelve operational CRACs (Liberty model FH740C) were located around the perimeter of the room. The servers were located in a cold-aisle/hot-aisle arrangement, with aisle widths of approximately 4 ft (1.2 m). The cold aisles were populated with 40% open tiles (Macaccess model AL series). A hot aisle displaying the rows of racks is shown in Figure 2.13. Since this was a test environment, no covers were installed on any of the server racks.

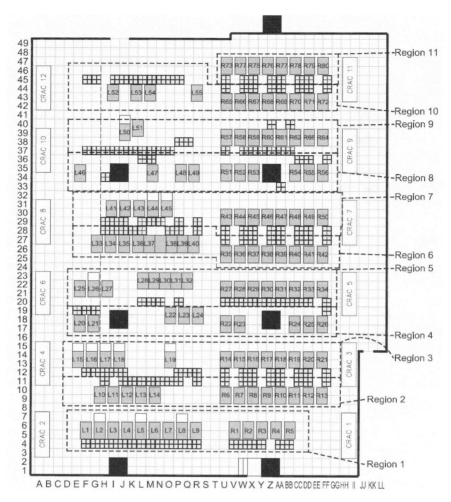

Figure 2.10 IBM Poughkeepsie (2004) datacom equipment layout.

MEASUREMENT TOOLS

The airflow through the perforated floor tiles, cable cut-outs, and CRACs was measured with a velometer. The unit was calibrated in a wind tunnel, and all measurements were adjusted based on the calibration (the velometer was measuring approximately 4% and 7% low for the range of airflows measured on the 500 and 1000 cfm scales, respectively). In addition to this correction, the reading of the velometer was also corrected for the reduction in airflow caused by the unit's flow

Figure 2.11 Isolation of the measurement area under floor partitions (top) and above floor partitions (bottom).

impedance. The unit was modeled using a CFD software package, where the resulting correction is given by the following:

Corrected flow for 500 cfm scale (cfm) =
1.11 × measured flow rate (cfm) − 16.6

Corrected flow for 1000 cfm scale (cfm) =
1.14 × measured flow rate (cfm) − 16.6

The results presented in the remainder of this case study include the above corrections.

The temperatures were measured with a handheld Omega HH23 meter using a type T thermocouple. Since temperature differences and not absolute temperatures were most important, the meter was not calibrated, although the error in the thermocouple and instrument was estimated to be ±1.8°F (±1.0°C). Temperature difference errors were estimated to be ±1.8°F (±1.0°C), resulting primarily from cycling of the CRACs.

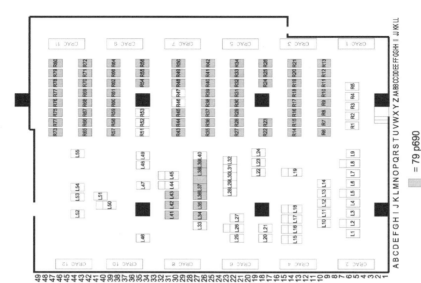

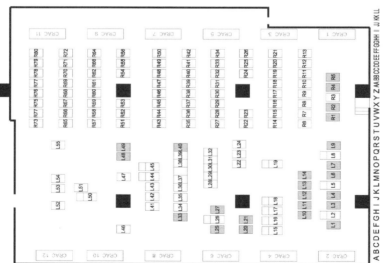

Figure 2.12 Identification of frames.

Figure 2.13 Row of racks in the hot aisle.

The input power of most of the racks was measured by connecting a laptop with custom software to the server. For comparison, another tool was connected inline to the cable used to power the server. The comparisons between the two power measurement tools were within 3% for the two systems measured. For ease of measurement, the tool that was connected to the input power of the rack was used throughout the data center.

MEASUREMENT METHODOLOGY AND RESULTS

Power Measurements

A good estimate of the total power dissipated in the data center was determined since the power of most of the racks was measured. A summary of all the powers are summarized in Table 2.2. As shown, the electronic equipment dissipated 1088 kW. All electronic racks operate with a power factor correction of nearly 1.0 with three-phase 208 V input to the racks. For those few racks that could not be measured, the power profile of each piece of equipment was used to estimate power dissipation. These racks only contributed 8% to the overall power dissipated by the electronic equipment. The error in the estimated rack powers was considered to be ±15%, while those of the measured rack powers were ±3%, giving a combined error of ±3%. The

Table 2.2   Power Information

Equipment	Power, kW
Total CRACs	**71.4**
Total Lighting (94 Fixtures)	**9.5**
Region 1	247.6
Region 2	100.7
Region 3	88.4
Region 4	65.6
Region 5	120.6
Region 6	123.3
Region 7	89.1
Region 8	43.0
Region 9	70.4
Region 10	84.1
Region 11	55.9
Total Electronics	**1088.7**
Total Data Center Load	**1169.6**

rack input powers are displayed as bar graphs in Figures 2.14–2.18. Due to space limitations, not all regions are shown, but the ones shown are representative.

The CRACs and lighting also contribute to the overall heat load in the data center. Since none of the CRACs had humidification or reheat capabilities, the only power expenditure was that of a 10 hp blower. This power value was used for all the CRACs except three that exhausted significantly less airflow. For these, the pumping power (based on measured CRAC flow described in the next section) was used to estimate the power dissipated by these units. These data are also summarized in Table 2.2. Lighting was provided by T12 Mark III-Energy Saver fluorescent fixtures rated at 101 W each. With 94 fixtures in this portion of the data center, the resulting total lighting heat load was 9.5 kW. Therefore, the total heat load in the data center was 1170 kW. The maximum error in the total heat load value was estimated to be ±3%.

Airflow Measurements

The airflow from the perforated floor tiles was measured with a velometer. This flow tool fits exactly over one perforated tile and provides an excellent means of rapidly profiling the flow throughout the data center. Measured flows from each tile or cable cut-out were very stable, varying by <10 cfm (0.28 m^3/min). The measured flow rates from each perforated tile are also shown in Figures 2.14–2.18.

Measuring the cable cut-out airflows could not be achieved directly since it was impossible to position the flow tool directly over the cable cut-out due to cable

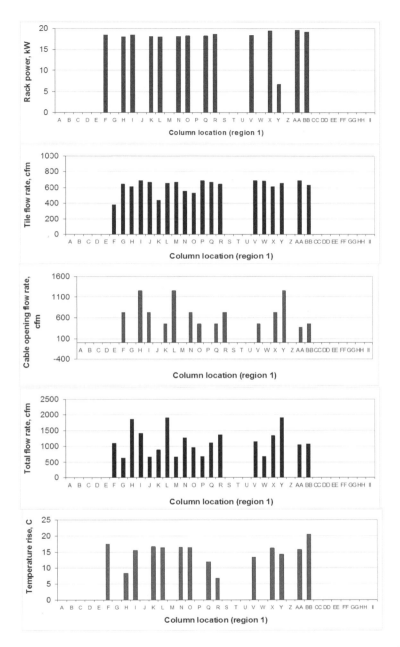

Figure 2.14 Environmental characteristics of racks in region 1 (see Figure 2.10).

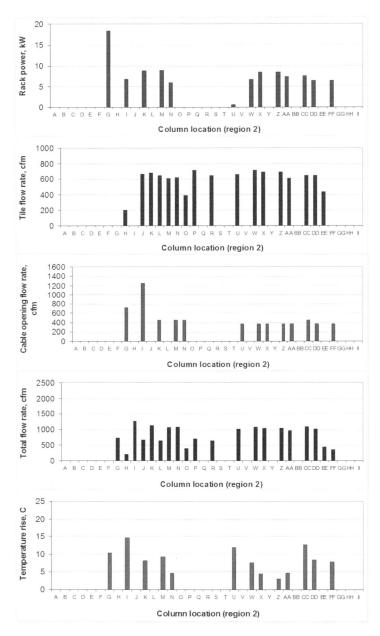

Figure 2.15 Environmental characteristics of racks in region 2 (see Figure 2.10).

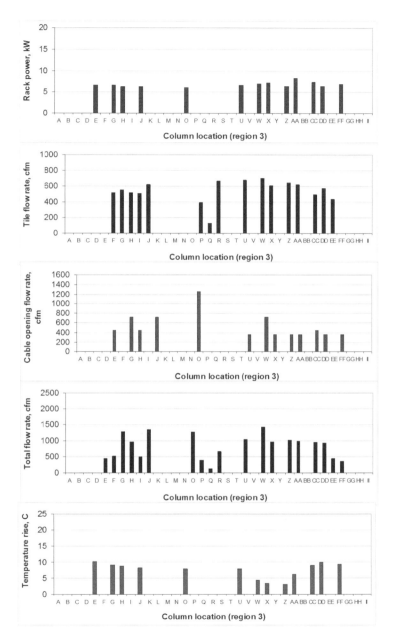

Figure 2.16 Environmental characteristics of racks in region 3 (see Figure 2.10).

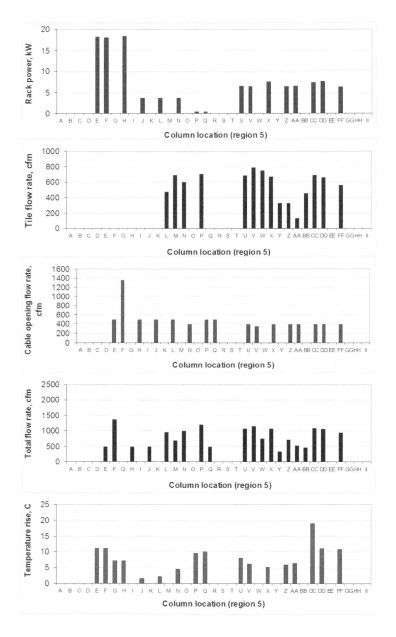

Figure 2.17 Environmental characteristics of racks in region 5 (see Figure 2.10).

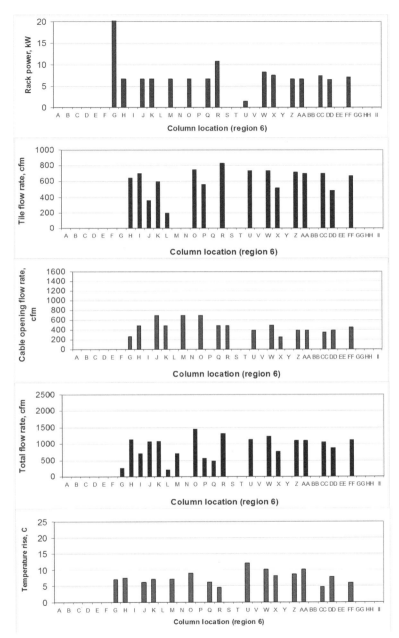

Figure 2.18 Environmental characteristics of racks in region 6 (see Figure 2.10).

interference. To eliminate this interference, a short, rectangular, open-ended box with a small cut-out on the side for the cables to enter was installed on the bottom of the instrument. The airflow measurements from the cable cut-outs are also shown in Figures 2.14–2.18. Measurements were made of a select number of cable cut-outs that included all the various sizes distributed throughout the raised-access floor. In addition, the static pressures were measured at select locations. Based on the static pressure measurements and the measured airflow through the cable cut-outs, estimates were made of the remaining cut-out airflow rates.

The overall airflow of the data center was based on all the measurements and estimations of flow from the perforated floor tiles and cable cut-outs. The sum of these measurements was 151,145 cfm (4280 m^3/min) after adjusting for the calibration in the flowmeter. One additional area of flow not accounted for was the leakage of air that occurred between the perforated tiles. This leakage occurred since the perforated tiles did not fit tightly together (small air gaps exist for air to escape). Tate Access Floors (2004) states that a typical air leakage is 0.69 cfm/ft^2 (0.21 m^3/ min/m^2) at a static pressure of 0.05 in. (1.27 mm) of water gauge. Since measurements beneath the floor showed underfloor static pressures of approximately 0.09 in. (2.29 mm) of water, the estimated air leakage was estimated to be 0.92 cfm/ ft^2(0.28 m^3/min/m^2). As the data center had an area of 7450 ft^2 (692 m^2), the total air leakage was estimated to be 6,850 cfm (194 m^3/min). This resulted in a total estimated data center airflow rate of 157,995 cfm (4473.8 m^3/min). The estimated error in the total data center flow rate was estimated to be 4.8% (10% for cable cut-outs and 4% for perforated floor tiles).

The airflow through each CRAC was difficult to measure since there was no easy way to obtain the nonuniform, highly turbulent airflow exhausting the CRAC beneath the floor. Nor was it easy to obtain the total flow entering the CRAC at its inlet. The estimated flow through the CRACs was 13,166 cfm (372.8 m^3/min) (157,995 cfm per 12 CRACs [4474 m^3/min per 12 CRACs]). However, each CRAC demonstrated some differences in flow due to backpressures under the floor, filter cleanliness differences, variations in the unit, etc. To obtain some estimate of the variation in airflow between the units, the velometer was employed. A grid of flow measurements was taken across the inlet face of the CRAC and used to tabulate the average velocity. From the average velocity and area, the total airflow into the CRAC was computed. First, the velometer was placed above the CRAC at the inlet to measure a portion of the flow entering the unit. Obviously the flow was not the same, since the opening into the top of the tool (14 × 14 in. [355.6 × 355.6 mm]) was not the same as the bottom (23 × 23 in. [584.2 × 584.2 mm]). With measurements at six locations, these were averaged and multiplied by the area of the inlet of the CRAC. These measurements were then used to proportion the flow among the CRACs, the estimates of which are shown in Table 2.3 for each CRAC. The CRAC airflow stated in the manufacturer's catalog for this model unit (Liebert model FH740C) is 16,500 cfm (467.2 m^3/min).

Table 2.3   CRAC Information

Unit ID	Flow Rate, cfm	Return Temp., °C	Supply Temp., °C	Cooling, kW	Power Consumption, kW
CRAC 01	4873	30.6	11.8	47.8	1.0
CRAC 02	8967	28.5	11.8	78.1	1.6
CRAC 03	14946	26.2	11.8	112.2	2.2
CRAC 04	15224	27.3	11.8	123.0	7.4
CRAC 05	14667	25.0	11.8	100.9	7.4
CRAC 06	15061	24.8	11.8	102.1	7.4
CRAC 07	14946	22.0	11.8	79.5	7.4
CRAC 08	13840	23.0	11.8	80.8	7.4
CRAC 09	14946	24.7	11.8	100.5	7.4
CRAC 10	15056	22.0	11.8	80.0	7.4
CRAC 11	15503	23.4	11.8	93.7	7.4
CRAC 12	9967	22.3	11.8	54.5	7.4
Total Cooling				**1053.2**	

Temperature Measurements

Temperatures were measured of the supply air exhausting the perforated floor tiles, the air inlet into the racks at a height of 68.9 in. (1750 mm), and the return air to the CRACs. The temperature differences between the raised-access floor supply air and the air entering the rack at a height of 68.9 in. (1750 mm) is shown in Figures 2.14–2.18. These temperatures were taken 2 in. (50 mm) in front of the covers in accordance with ASHRAE (2004) guidelines. The graph of the rise in inlet air temperatures for each rack is shown at the bottom of each figure. Return air temperatures at the each CRAC were also measured (see Table 2.3).

ANALYSIS AND COMPARISONS

Thermal Profiles

As in Section 2.1.1, the airflow through the cable cut-outs is significant—approximately half of the total flow was from cable cut-outs and leakage through the tiles. Although the flow from the cable cut-outs provided some cooling, the analysis by Schmidt and Cruz (2002) shows this is not the best use of the supply air from the raised-access floor. If the hot exhaust air exiting the racks is drawn back into the inlet of the rack, then the chilled air exhausting the cable cut-outs cools this exhaust air before it enters into the front of the racks. It is more efficient if no air exhausts from the cable openings and all is exhausted from the cold aisle.

The supply air from the perforated floor tiles adjacent to the IBM p690 racks, along with the corresponding temperature rise to the inlet of the racks, is depicted in Figure 2.19. The average airflow rate from perforated tiles adjacent to the p690 racks was 516 cfm (14.6 m^3/min) for the data center. The average temperature rise to the inlet of the racks at a height of 68.9 in. (1750 mm) from the raised-access floor was 15.8°F (8.8°C). The tile flow rate for the p690s in Schmidt (2004) was 342 cfm (9.5 m^3/min), and the temperature rise was 18.9°F (10.5°C). Finally, the chilled airflow rates stated here should be compared to the airflow rate through the rack, which was approximately 1050 cfm (29.7 m^3/min). Since each rack extended 1.25 tiles in width, the total flow to the face of a rack was assumed to be an average of 645 cfm (18.3 m^3/min) (1.25 × 516 cfm or 1.25 × 13.6 m^3/min). Since the airflow rate through each p690 rack was approximately 1050 cfm (29.7 m^3/min), it is obvious that the airflow rate from the perforated tile adjacent to the rack was less than the flow through the rack. Since the temperature rise to the top of the rack averaged 15.8°F (8.8°C), the temperature plume exhausting the rear of the racks mixed with the air in a larger region, thereby damping the temperature rise. This suggests that there was enough mixing in the room to bring the exhaust temperatures down even though the local airflow rates were much lower than what might be considered adequate. This was similar to the results obtained from Schmidt (2004). The average temperature rise for the p655 racks (average power 19 kW) was 20.3°F (11.3°C), as displayed in Figure 2.19.

The entire data center had a heat flux of 157 W/ft^2 (14.6 W/m^2), based on the total area. However, in one area (portions of regions 1 and 2), as highlighted in Figure 2.20, the heat flux was 512 W/ft^2 (5500 W/m^2). Since the racks were approximately 1.25 tiles wide, the total perforated tile airflow associated with the rack in this area was approximately 750 cfm (21.2 m^3/min), which is about one-third of the airflow rate through the rack. The airflow rate through the p655 racks was approximately 2400 cfm (68 m^3/min). Schmidt (2004) noted that if the perforated tile airflow was in the range of one-quarter to one-half of the rack airflow, with underfloor air temperatures between 50°F–59°F (10°C–15°C), then the air inlet temperature could be met. The cable cut-out airflow rate in this area associated with each rack was approximately 800 cfm (22.6 m^3/min). This meant that the total airflow in the region of a rack in this area was approximately 1600 cfm, compared to 2400 cfm (68.0 m^3/min) through the rack. Again, one-half to two-thirds of the airflow was needed to satisfy the rack inlet temperature requirements as long as the total heat load at the facility level was accommodated.

Energy Balance

To confirm the accuracy of the data, two different comparison of the power were made. One was based on the mass flow rate through the CRACs and their associated temperature difference across the unit. The second was the measured total power of all the systems within the data center. These comparisons are shown in Tables 2.2–2.3. The supply temperatures from the CRACs were based on an average of the ten

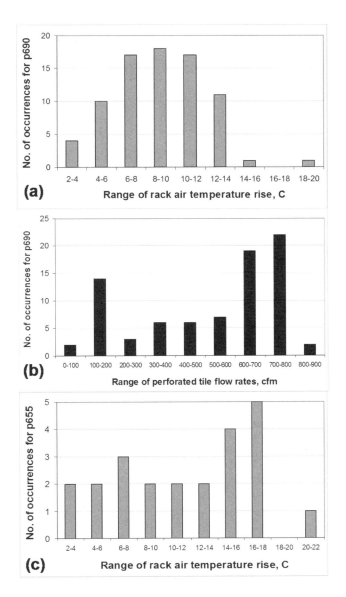

Figure 2.19 Statistical analysis of various parameters: (a) rack inlet temperature rise for the 79 p690 machines (average 15.8°F [8.8°C]), (b) perforated tile flow rates in front of p690 machines (average 516 cfm [14.6 m³/min]), and (c) rack inlet temperature rise for the 23 p655 machines (average 20.3°F [11.3°C]).

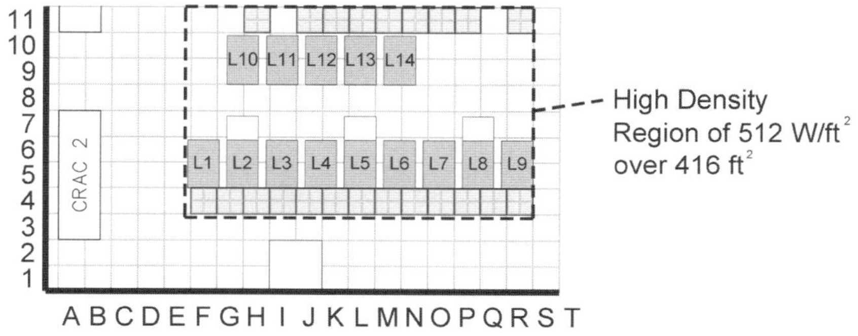

Figure 2.20 High density region in the data center.

lowest exit air temperatures from the perforated tiles with the assumption that these were representative of the supply temperature from the CRAC units. The measured power shown in Table 2.3 is 1169.6 kW ±3% (1134–1204 kW). The calculated power based on the mass flow rate and the temperature difference across the CRAC units is 1053.2 kW ±9.8% (950–1156 kW). A comparison of these values shows excellent agreement and closure on an energy balance.

SUMMARY

A methodology similar to Schmidt's (2004) was outlined and described with the aid of measurements collected from a high density data center. The components of the measurements included the following:

- Power
  - ✓ Racks
  - ✓ Lighting
  - ✓ CRAC

- Temperatures
  - ✓ Rack inlet air
  - ✓ CRAC return air
  - ✓ Supply air from perforated floor tiles

- Airflows
  - ✓ CRAC
  - ✓ Perforated floor tiles
  - ✓ Cable cut-outs

These measurements allowed a detailed thermal profile of the data center.

As in Schmidt (2004), the flow rate from the perforated tile in front of the rack is less than that flowing through the rack. In most cases, this is one-quarter to one-half of the flow rate through the rack. This was the case for both the p690 racks, which dissipated approximately 7 kW (with a rack flow rate of 1100 cfm [31.1 m^3/min]) and the p655, which dissipated approximately 19 kW (with a rack flow rate of 2400 cfm (68 m^3/min]). If the cable cut-outs are included, the combined flow was in the range of one-half to two-thirds of the rack flow rate, similar to that reported in Schmidt (2004). Even though the local flow rate adjacent to the racks did not appear adequate, the convection currents that occurred at the room level were sufficient to bring the local air temperatures for the high-powered racks within the temperature specifications.

An energy balance was performed using two different methods, and both showed excellent agreement.

This case study describes a specific set of measurements from a high density data center in order to provide details of the thermal profile. In addition, the data collection techniques described can be used as a basis for collecting data from other data centers or telecom rooms and provide a presentation format in which to display the information.

REFERENCES

ASHRAE. 2004. *Thermal Guidelines for Data Processing Environments*. Atlanta: American Society of Heating, Refrigerating and Air-Conditioning Engineers, Inc.

Schmidt, R.R. 2004. Thermal profile of a high density data center—Methodology to thermally characterize a data center. *ASHRAE Transactions* 110(2):635–42.

Schmidt, R., and E. Cruz. 2002. Raised floor computer data center: Effect on rack inlet temperatures of exiting both the hot and cold aisle. *Proceedings of Itherm Conference 2002, San Diego, CA,* pp. 580–94.

Tate Access Floors. 2004. Controlling air leakage from raised access floor cavities. Technical Bulletin #216, Tate Access Floors, Inc., Jessup, MD.

2.1.3   CASE STUDY 3—SAN DIEGO SUPERCOMPUTER CENTER

This case study characterizes an 11,490 ft^2 (1067 m^2) high density data center, focusing on a zone with heat dissipation greater than 8 kW, up to 26 kW per frame. To gain insight into the operational health of the data center, a survey is conducted that measures power consumption, airflow, and temperature. The results are analyzed using a CFD model. The methodology used here is similar to that used in the NCEP data center case study (Schmidt 2004).

LAYOUT OF DATA CENTER

The San Diego Supercomputer Center (SDSC) is located on the University of California San Diego campus. The data center area is 88 × 140 ft (26.8 × 42.7 m); however, the area available for CRACs, power distribution panels, and IT equipment is 11,490 ft^2 (1067 m^2). Figure 2.21 shows an overall plan view with the focus zone highlighted. The IT equipment installed in the outlined zone is as follows: a 7039-651 IBM eServer pSeries 655 server model 651, an IBM eServer pSeries 690, and a 7045-SW4 IBM eServer pSeries high-performance switch (HPS) model SW4. The data center slab-to-slab height is 16 ft (4.9 m), broken down as follows: 2 ft. (0.6 m) concrete subfloor to raised-access floor, 10 ft (3.0 m) raised-access floor to suspended ceiling, and 4 ft (1.2 m) above the suspended ceiling. Selected ceiling panels are removed in the hot aisles to facilitate IT equipment exhaust air to the CRACs with return duct extensions, as shown in Figure 2.22. The CRACs also have turning vanes installed.

A hot-aisle/cold-aisle arrangement is used throughout the data center with varying aisle pitch (distance from the center of one cold aisle to the center of the next cold aisle) ranging from 7–10 raised-access floor panels. All panels are 2 × 2 ft (0.6 × 0.6 m). The perforated raised-access floor panels are estimated to be 22% open, based on the diameter of each hole and the hole pattern. There are several underfloor blockages from insulated chilled-water supply and return pipes, as well as from cable bundles and cable trays (see Figures 2.23–2.24).

MEASUREMENT TOOLS

The airflow through the perforated panels is measured with an Alnor Balometer capture hood. Because the capture hood obstructs the airflow from the perforated panel, the cfm readings must be adjusted by a correction factor. However, the Alnor capture hood has a built-in back pressure compensation feature via a flap that accounts for the flow impedance of the capture hood. The feature is used for every measured perforated panel. Measurement accuracy based on the manufacturer's specification sheet is ±3% of the airflow reading. Cable cut-outs are measured with a wind vane with anemometer air-velocity meter. Measurement accuracy, based on the manufacturer's data sheet, is ±2% of the velocity reading. Temperature measurements of the IT equipment air intakes are made with an Omega model HH23 digital thermometer with a type T thermocouple. Measurement accuracy, based on the

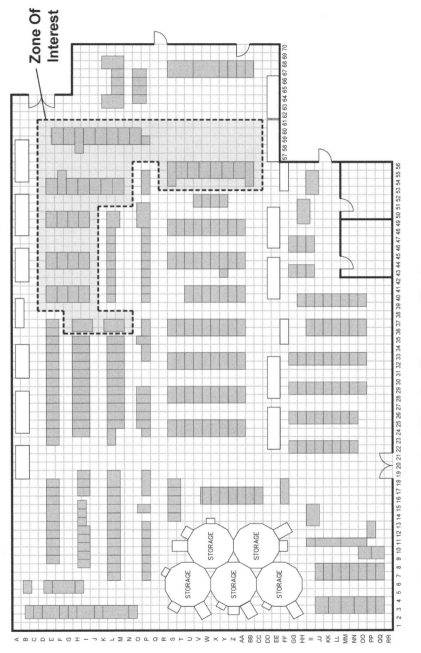

Figure 2.21 Data center layout with additional profile zone outlined.

Figure 2.22 CRACs with return-air duct extensions.

Figure 2.23 Under raised-access floor blockage.

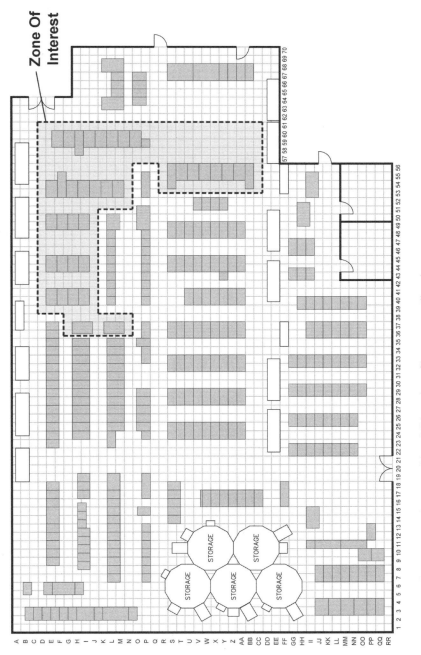

Figure 2.21 Data center layout with additional profile zone outlined.

Figure 2.22 CRACs with return-air duct extensions.

Figure 2.23 Under raised-access floor blockage.

Figure 2.24 Under raised-access floor blockage.

manufacturer's product specification, is ±0.1% of the temperature reading. All test equipment cited is calibrated on a yearly basis to ISO/IEC 17025 (ISO/IEC 2005).

All voltage and current measurements are provided by the staff at SDSC. The amperage data by circuit supplied by SDSC is measured with a Fluke T5-600 electrical tester and a Fluke 33 clamp meter. The instruments are not calibrated, but the input power to several frames was also checked for comparison. A laptop with custom communications software is connected to an interface on the frame, and the percent difference is <5%.

MEASUREMENTS AND RESULTS

Power Measurements

The heat load of the data center, including the IT equipment, CRACs, and lighting, is collected on-site with the help of SDSC personnel. The IT equipment in the data center is supplied by 208 volts of alternating current (VAC), either three-phase or line-to-line, and 120 VAC line-to-neutral. The CRACs are supplied with 480 VAC line-to-line. Table 2.4 shows a breakdown of the power dissipation. The CRACs have a range of heat output that varies significantly. The heat output of the IT equipment is calculated from the sum of the amperages multiplied by the associated mains connection. The result is volt-amps (VA), but a power factor of 0.95 is provided by SDSC to determine

Table 2.4   Total Data Center Power Dissipation

Equipment	Power, kW
CRACs	
CCU 01	15.8
CCU 02	23.3
CCU 03	7.5
CCU 04	7.3
CCU 05	14.1
CCU 06	8.1
CCU 07	10.0
CCU 08	10.8
CCU 09	14.1
CCU 10	10.8
CCU 11	14.1
CCU 12	19.1
Total CRAC Power	**155.1**
Total Lights	**15.0**
Power Panels	
CL1U	426.2
U3	55.5
RDC	595.7
U4	175.7
SATA	53.1
GG	39.5
Total Power Panels	**1345.7**
Total Power Consumption	**1515.8**

the watts, as most IT equipment has active mitigation to comply with the harmonics emissions standard 61000-3-2 (IEC 2005). However, it is important to note that all the IBM p690 and p655 three-phase servers, which are a significant load in the data center and are not within the scope of 61000-3-2, include active mitigation and have a power factor very close to one. Table 2.5 shows a breakdown of the zone with the high density servers. The numbers in parentheses are the quantity of IBM server racks. The maximum error in the total heat load is estimated to be ±5%.

Several p655s are measured directly at the frame through a communications interface on the bulk power system. The measurements compare favorably to the

Table 2.5   Select IT Power Dissipation

IT Equipment	Power, kW
p690 (11)	91.4
p655 (18)	420.9
HPS (6)	46.3
Total Power Consumption	**558.6**

data from the power panels, although the power panels are consistently higher by <5%. This result is most likely due to measurement error with uncalibrated instruments and distribution losses.

Airflow Measurements and Modeling

There are a total of 12 Liebert Deluxe System/3 chilled-water CRACs installed on the raised-access floor. Table 2.6 provides the manufacturer specifications for each individual CRAC. The sensible cooling is calculated based on a return air temperature of 73°F (22.8°C) dry bulb, a return air relative humidity (RH) of 37%, a supply water temperature of 41°F (5°C), and a return water temperature to the chiller of 53°F (11.7°C). The return air data are collected from the Liebert monitoring system and averaged as the temperature and humidity sensors are located as shown in Table 2.6. The method in case study 1 used to measure airflow through each CRAC could not be used because of the return duct extensions, and there was not enough time during our study to perform a rectangular duct velocity traverse via the Equal Area or the Log Tchebycheff method (Richardson 2001). However, the results from TileFlow®, a CFD tool for simulating airflow and temperature distribution in raised-access floor environments, indicate that the actual airflow is within the measurement tolerance of the manufacturer-specified airflow. The TileFlow results are discussed at the end of this section.

The data center has a total of 233 perforated panels. The total open area is 200 ft^2 (18.6 m^2), based on 22% open perforated panels. Each perforated panel is measured via the Alnor capture hood with back pressure compensation, and the airflow is recorded. The total volumetric airflow from the 233 perforated panels is 99,947 cfm (2830 m^3/min). The data center also has a total of 306 cut-outs used for power and communications cable routing. The area of each opening is measured and adjusted for the estimated cable blockage. The total open area is 92 ft^2 (8.5 m^2). Because of time constraints, only 17 openings are measured using the anemometer with wind vane.

The data collected on the CRACs, perforated panels, and cut-outs during the study are used to build a model in TileFlow and to compare the results to the measurements. In addition, significant underfloor blockages from cable trays, cable bundles, and chilled-water supply and return lines are added to the model. Also, the data center

Table 2.6   CRAC Detail

CRAC Number	Flow Rate, CFM	Sensible Cooling, kW	Sensor Location
MHB-CCU01	16,500	142	Power pillar 56
MHB-CCU02	16,500	142	Power pillar 56
MHB-CCU03	12,400	102	Return duct extension
MHB-CCU04	12,400	102	Return duct extension
MHB-CCU05	12,400	102	Return duct extension
MHB-CCU06	16,500	142	Power pillar 20
MHB-CCU07	16,500	142	Backside power pillar 54
MHB-CCU08	16,500	142	Backside power pillar 54
MHB-CCU09	16,500	142	Return duct extension
MHB-CCU10	16,500	142	Backside power pillar 54
MHB-CCU11	16,500	142	Return duct extension
MHB-CCU12	16,500	142	Power pillar 20
Total	**185,700**	**1582**	

is spot checked for perimeter openings in the raised-access floor cavity. None are revealed, although an exhaustive review was not done. Finally, the distributed leakage area of air between perforated panels is estimated to be 0.2%, based on the average width of the gaps between floor panels. Typical percent leakage area values can range from 0.1% to 0.2% but can be as high as 0.35% (Radmehr et al. 2005). The model is run several times with different distributed leakage values to arrive at an acceptable comparison between measured and predicted values. However, the leakage may be larger than assumed since the data center has been in existence for some time and there are areas of high static pressure as high as 0.094 in. wg. All in all, there is only a 1.7% difference in total cfm between measured and simulated airflows. Figure 2.25 shows the measured versus modeled results on a perforated panel-by-panel basis. The average static pressure for the entire raised floor is 0.048 in. wg.

Initial runs of the model showed some wide excursions because of dampers that are used on some of the perforated panels. Since the measured airflow rates are available and the pressure drop usually varies as the square of the airflow rate, it is possible to refine the model. The additional airflow resistance is entered in the polynomial expression for a particular perforated panel, and the model is rerun. The airflow from the perforated panels in row AA of Figure 2.21, closest to CRACs CCU8–12, show the largest discrepancy between measured and modeled values, but perforated panels in adjacent rows show good correlation.

A comparison of the cut-outs shows good correlation between measured and modeled data for openings less than 25 in.^{2} (161 cm^2). The percent difference is <15%. The larger cut-out comparison shows that the predicted volumetric airflow is significantly higher than the measured airflow. The reason for the discrepancy most

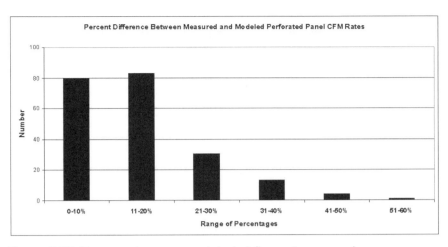

Figure 2.25 Measured versus modeled airflow rate comparison.

likely has to do with the measurement technique. Regardless of the size of the cut-out, three measurements are taken to obtain data in the shortest amount of time. Because the wind vane area is 5 in.^{2} (32 cm^2), it is very difficult to obtain a representative linear airflow with three readings of a large opening, for example 100 in.^{2} (645 cm^2), before integrating over the area.

Temperature Measurements

Temperatures are logged at the air intakes of the frames in the outlined zone shown in Figure 2.21. A single temperature reading is captured for each frame at a height of 68.9 in. (1750 mm) in accordance with ASHRAE guidelines (ASHRAE 2004) of 2 in. (50 mm) in front of the covers. The temperature of the air exiting each perforated panel supply airflow is measured by the capture hood and recorded. The return air to the CRACs could not be easily measured because of the return duct extensions. Instead, the CRAC sensor data are recorded.

High-Density Analysis. The gross density of air-conditioning capacity is 138 W/ft^2 (1485 W/m^2) and the current heat load density is 132 W/ft^2 (1421 W/m^2). Although this information is not particularly useful in the overall operational health evaluation, as it does not indicate airflow distribution problems, hot spots, etc., gross W/ft^2 is commonly used by real-estate operations personnel in figuring data center costs. Table 2.7 gives a view of the total airflow in the data center with estimated accuracy.

Table 2.7 shows that approximately half of the airflow in the data center is from cut-outs and leakage. Although there may be some benefit to cooling of IT equipment, prior studies (Schmidt and Cruz 2002a) show that the cut-out air is heated by the IT exhaust air before returning to the IT air intakes.

Table 2.7   Data Center Airflow

Airflow	cfm	Notes	Accuracy
Total volumetric flow	185,700	Liebert specifications	10%
Perforated panels	99,947	Measured	5%
Cut-outs	75,156	Calculated with approximate blockages	15%
Leakage	10,597	0.2% distributed area in the model	5%

The frame power, airflow rates, and inlet temperatures for the zone outlined in Figure 2.21 are examined similarly to those in case study 1. The zone is divided into three sections for further study. The environmental characteristics are shown in Figures 2.26–2.30.

Figures 2.26–2.30 show that the air intake temperatures are within or below the ASHRAE Class 1 recommended dry-bulb temperature range of 68°F–76°F (20°C–25°C), regardless of frame power consumption and airflow rate through the IT equipment.

Table 2.8 shows a correlation between average perforated panel supply airflow, cut-out airflow, frame airflow, and frame temperature rise for a section and subsection. The average perforated pane supply airflow comes from the panels directly in front of the frames for this analysis, even though a cold aisle may be 4 ft (101.6 mm) wide. For comparison to the average frame airflow, the average perforated panel airflow is adjusted for the frame width of 1.25 panels. The frame airflows are as follows: 2960 cfm (83.8 m³/min) for the p655, 1100 cfm (31.1 m³/min) for the p690, and 800 cfm (22.7 m³/min) for the switch frames. The frame temperature rise is calculated based on the difference between the average temperature of the air exiting a given row of perforated panels and the aggregate return air temperature of the CRAC sensors within the vicinity of that row.

Table 2.8 shows that the airflow rates from the perforated panels in front of the frames are much less than the frame airflow rates. Despite the imbalance in airflow, air-intake temperatures are within or below ASHRAE Class 1 recommendations, as shown in Figures 2.26–2.30. If the perforated panel and cut-out adjacent to a frame are combined to provide the airflow, the calculated temperature rise based on average frame power is shown in Table 2.9.

The calculated temperature rise in Table 2.9 is higher than the actual temperature rise in Table 2.8 for each section. Therefore, the conclusion is the same as that for case study 1: chilled air within the data center migrates from low-density to high-density zones, as the local chilled airflow rates for the high-density frames are much lower than what might be considered adequate.

Airflow Comparison. An airflow comparison is made between the actual airflow, and a calculated airflow from the data center measured heat load and temperature difference. The actual airflow, based on perforated panel measurements, limited cable cut-out measurements, and modeling, is 185,700 cfm (5258 m³/min), with an estimated accuracy of 10% derived from various simulation results. The actual airflow range is 167,130–204,270 cfm (4732–5784 m³/min). The average temperature difference from

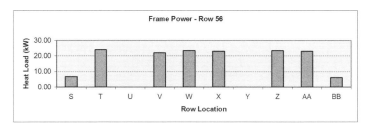

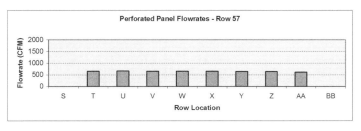

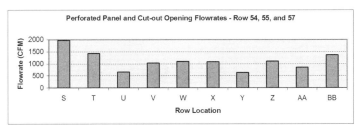

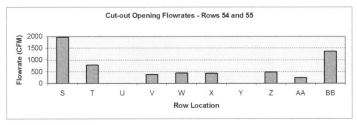

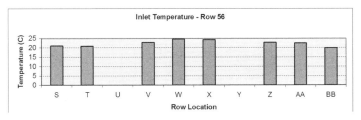

Figure 2.26 Environmental characteristics of frames in section 1.

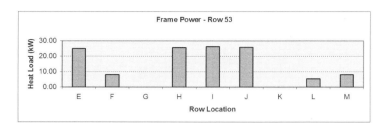

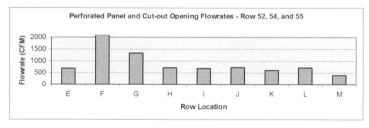

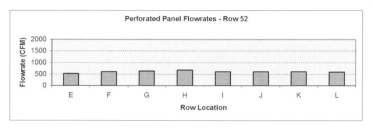

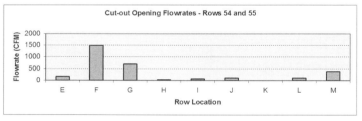

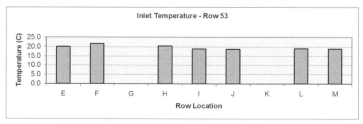

Figure 2.27 Environmental characteristics of frames in section 2(1).

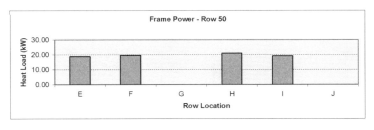

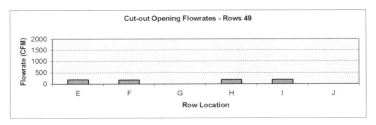

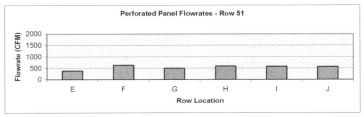

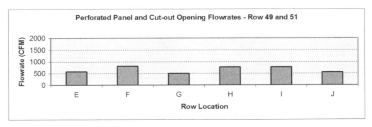

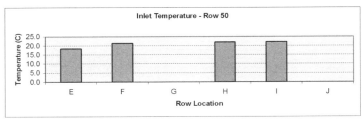

Figure 2.28 Environmental characteristics of frames in section 2(2).

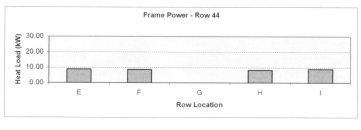

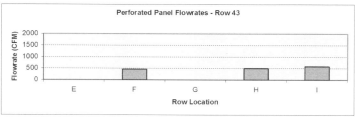

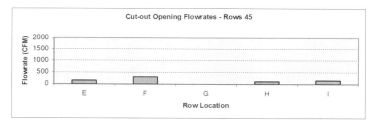

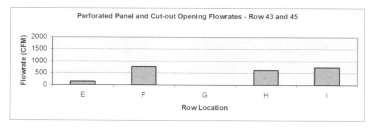

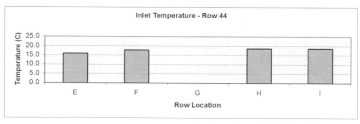

Figure 2.29 Environmental characteristics of frames in section 3(1).

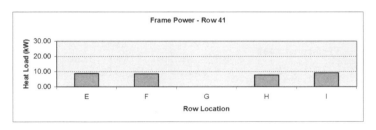

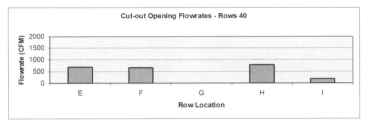

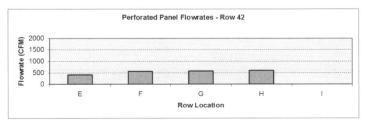

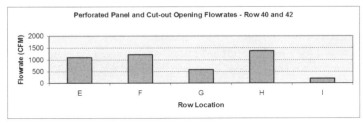

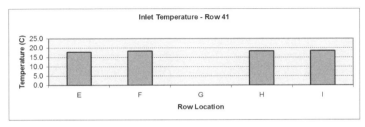

Figure 2.30 Environmental characteristics of frames in section 3(2).

Table 2.8   Section Analysis of Airflow and Temperature Rise

Section Number	Average Perforated Panel Airflow, cfm	Average Cut-Out Airflow, cfm	Average Frame Airflow cfm	Average Frame Temp. Rise °C
1	645	762	2420	12.9
2 (1)	672	386	2077	12.0
2 (2)	816	189	2960	12.4
3 (1)	390	182	1100	11.4
3 (2)	537	584	1025	11.7

Table 2.9   Calculation of Average Frame Temperature Rise

Section Number	Average Perforated Panel and Cut-Out Airflow, CFM	Average Frame Power Consumption, kW	Calculated Average Frame Temp. Rise, °C
1	1408	19.0	23.8
2(1)	1057	17.8	29.6
2(2)	1005	19.7	34.5
3(1)	571	8.7	26.7
3(2)	1121	8.6	13.5

perforated panel temperature measurements and CRAC sensors is 27°F (15°C), with an estimated error of 10%. The total heat load accuracy is estimated to be ±5%. The calculated airflow is 177,664 cfm (5031 m^3/min), with a range of 153,437–207,205 cfm (4345–5867 m^3/min). There is good overlap in the actual and calculated airflow ranges; therefore, the comparison of the data are validated.

SUMMARY

This case study presents a detailed characterization of a high density data center. On-site measurements of heat load, airflow, and temperature are measured and collected to study the data center. These parameters are used to build a CFD model and run simulations to provide detail on parameters, such as cut-out and leakage airflow, which could not be captured during the study either because of time or physical constraints. The model is validated based on the comparison between perforated panel measurements and the results of the model, as the total airflow percent difference is only 2%. An airflow comparison also confirms that the actual airflow and calculated airflow are in agreement.

The high density area of the data center with IBM equipment is studied. The key IT equipment health indicator is the inlet temperature, which is within or below the ASHRAE Class 1 guideline, even though the sum of the perforated panel and cut-out airflow rates are up to two-thirds less than the frame airflow rates. While the local conditions do not seem adequate to satisfy and maintain the air intake temperatures of the high-powered frames, the overall data center flow rate can handle the total data center heat load. However, as more high-density equipment is installed, there is a risk of locally elevated inlet temperatures, even though there may be sufficient cooling capacity. The conclusions for case study 3 and case study 1 are similar.

REFERENCES

ASHRAE. 2004. *Thermal Guidelines for Data Processing Environments*. Atlanta: American Society of Heating, Refrigerating and Air-Conditioning Engineers, Inc.

IEC. 2005. Electromagnetic compatibility (EMC)—Part 3-2: Limits—Limits for harmonic current emissions (equipment input current ≤16A per phase). International Electrotechnical Commission, Geneva, Switzerland.

Radmehr, A., R. Schmidt, K. Karki, and S. Patankar. 2005. Distributed leakage flow in raised-floor data centers. *Proceedings of InterPACK 2005, San Francisco, California*, pp. 401–08.

Richardson, G. 2001. Traversing for accuracy in a rectangular duct. *Associated Air Balance Council Tab Journal* Summer 2001:20–27.

Schmidt, R.R. 2004. Thermal profile of a high density data center—Methodology to thermally characterize a data center. *ASHRAE Transactions* 110(2):635–42.

Schmidt, R., and E. Cruz. 2002a. Raised floor computer data center: Effect on rack inlet temperatures of exiting both the hot and cold aisle. *Proceedings of Itherm Conference 2002, San Diego, CA*, pp. 580–94.

TileFlow, trademark of Innovative Research, Inc., Plymouth, Minnesota.

2.1.4 CASE STUDY 4—
IBM TEST FACILITY IN POUGHKEEPSIE (2005)

This case study and case study 5 describes the thermal profile of a high-performance computing cluster located, at different times, in two different data centers with different thermal profiles. The high-performance Advanced Simulation and Computing (ASC) cluster, developed and manufactured by IBM, is code named *ASC Purple*. It is the world's third-fastest supercomputer, operating at a peak performance of 77.8 TFlop/s. ASC Purple, which employs IBM pSeries p575, model 9118, contains more than 12,000 processors, 50 terabytes of memory, and 2 petabytes of globally accessible disk space. The cluster was first tested in the IBM development lab in Poughkeepsie, New York, and then shipped to Lawrence Livermore National Labs in Livermore, California, where it was installed to support our national security mission. Detailed measurements were taken in both data centers of electronic equipment power usage, perforated floor tile airflow, cable cut-out airflow, CRAC airflow, and electronic equipment inlet air temperatures. In addition to these measurements, the physical features of the data center were recorded. Results showed that heat fluxes of 700 W/ft^2 (7535 W/m^2) could be achieved while still maintaining rack inlet air temperatures within specifications. However, in some areas of the Poughkeepsie data center, there were zones that did exceed the equipment inlet air temperature specifications by a significant amount. These areas will be highlighted and reasons given why these areas failed to meet the criteria. Those areas of the cluster in Poughkeepsie that did not meet the temperature criteria were well within the temperature limits at the Livermore installation. Based on the results from these two data centers, necessary and sufficient criteria are outlined for IT racks to achieve inlet air temperatures that meet the manufacturers' temperature specifications.

LAYOUT OF DATA CENTER

The ASC Purple cluster was assembled for test verification in the IBM data center located at the IBM development lab in Poughkeepsie, New York. The data center is used to configure and test large clusters before shipping to a customer. The systems in this data center are located on a raised-access floor in an area approximately 70 × 240 ft (21 × 73 m). A plan view of the data center indicating the location of the CRACs is shown in Figure 2.31. Expanded views of the two regions shown in Figure 2.31 are displayed in Figures 2.32–2.33 along with the electronic racks and perforated tiles.

The area shown in Figures 2.31–2.33 for the cluster is part of a larger data center not shown in these pictures. In order to thermally isolate this area from other areas of the data center for the purposes of this study, several temporary partitions were installed. Plastic sheets were draped from the ceiling tiles to the floor near row 40 (in region B), shown in Figure 2.31. To further separate this area, the underfloor plenum

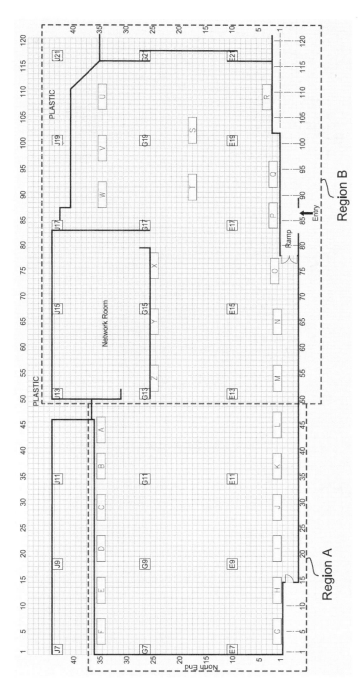

Figure 2.31 Overall IBM Poughkeepsie (2005) datacom equipment floor plan.

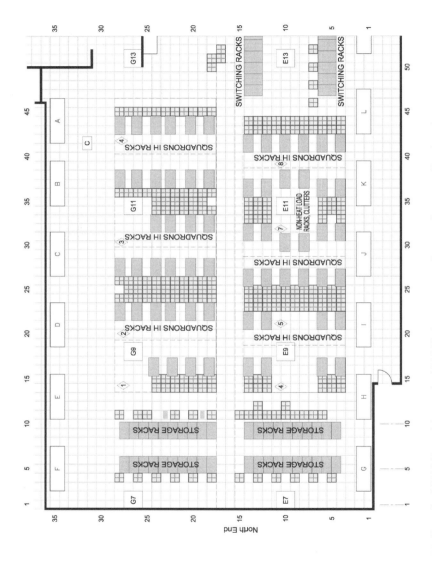

Figure 2.32 Detailed IBM Poughkeepsie (2005) datacom equipment layout—Region A.

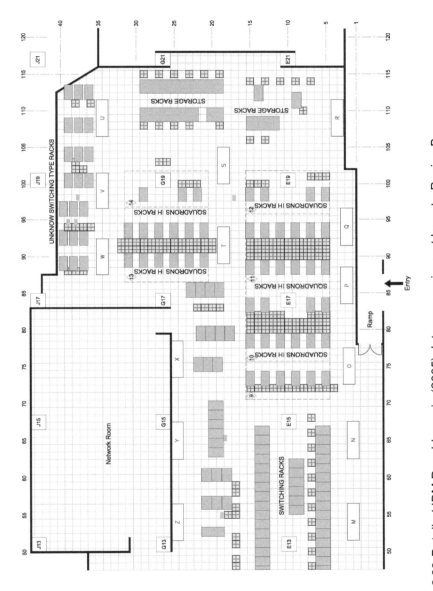

Figure 2.33 Detailed IBM Poughkeepsie (2005) datacom equipment layout—Region B.

was examined for openings around the perimeter of this portion of the room; where open areas existed, cardboard was used to block the airflow path. This transferred the entire heat load from the systems located in the area of interest to the CRACs.

The cluster was populated primarily with a high-powered server rack, p575 model 9118. The other systems were a mix of switching, communication, and storage equipment. The key classes of equipment are highlighted in Figures 2.32–2.33. The ceiling height as measured from the raised-access floor to the ceiling is 108 in. (2.74 m), with a raised-access floor height of 28 in. (0.7 m). Twenty-six operational Liebert model FH740C CRACs were primarily located around the perimeter of the room, as shown in Figure 2.31. The servers are located in a cold-aisle/hot-aisle arrangement with aisle widths of approximately 4 ft (1.2 m) and 6 ft (1.8 m). The cold aisles were populated with 40% open tiles. Since this is a test environment, no covers were installed on any of the server racks.

MEASUREMENT TOOLS

The airflow through the perforated floor tiles, cable cut-outs, and CRACs was measured with a commercial velometer. The unit was calibrated on a wind tunnel and all measurements were adjusted accordingly (the velometer measured approximately 4% and 7% low for the range of airflows measured with the 500 and 1000 cfm scales, respectively). In addition to this correction, the reading of the velometer also needed to be corrected for the reduction in airflow caused by the flow impedance of the unit. The unit was modeled using a CFD software package; the resulting correction for the unit is given by the following:

$$\text{Corrected flow for 500 cfm scale (cfm)} = 1.11 \times \text{measured flow rate (cfm)} - 16.6$$

$$\text{Corrected flow for 1000 cfm scale (cfm)} = 1.14 \times \text{measured flow rate (cfm)} - 16.6$$

The results presented in the remainder of this case study include the above corrections.

The temperatures were measured with a handheld meter using a type T thermocouple. Since temperature differences and not absolute temperatures were of most importance, the meter was not calibrated. The error in the thermocouple and instrument was estimated to be ±1.8°F (±1.0°C). Temperature difference errors were estimated to be ±1.8°F (±1.0°C), resulting primarily from cycling of the CRACs.

The input power of most of the racks was measured by connecting a laptop with custom software to the server to monitor the input power to the rack. For comparison, another tool was connected inline to the machine's power cable. The comparisons between the two power measurement tools were within 3% for the two systems measured. For ease of measurement, the tool that could be connected to the input power of the rack was used throughout the data center.

MEASUREMENTS AND RESULTS

The measurement methodology was very similar to that reported in the papers by Schmidt (2004) and Schmidt and Iyengar (2005b), with some exceptions. In order to adequately display the results of this study, the results were grouped by regions similarly to Schmidt and Iyengar (2005b), since the racks in these regions possessed similar thermal characteristics. For this study, the regions encompassed those racks that shared a common cold aisle. This allowed us to focus on the results much more quickly and highlight those areas that were of most interest. The following sections focus on the results of Table 2.10, as they refer to the fourteen regions highlighted in Figures 2.32 and 2.33.

Power Measurements

Since the power of all the server racks (p575) was measured, a good estimate of the total power dissipated from the cluster could be achieved. A summary of all the rack powers grouped by regions are summarized in Table 2.10. The electronic equipment dissipated 2.9 MW (with 1180 nodes operating). One node was a 2U server with up to 12 nodes installed in a rack. All electronic racks operated with a power factor correction of nearly 1.0 with three-phase 208 V input to the racks. For

Table 2.10   Thermal Profile of the IBM Poughkeepsie Data Center

Regions (See Figures 2.32–2.33)	Total Heat Dissipated, W	Area, ft²	Heat Flux, W/ft²	Average Rack Power, W	Average Rack Inlet Air Temp. °C	Average Chilled-Air Flowrate in Front of Rack, cfm/Rack
1	94,760	264	359	28,690	11.2	2166
2	293,196	462	635	24,433	22.9	1562
3	262,070	462	567	26,207	24.1	1392
4	158,472	264	600	26,412	23.6	959
5	103,540	242	428	25,885	13.9	1785
6	257,950	440	586	25,795	16.0	1573
7	206,784	440	470	25,848	20.6	1149
8	165,000	242	682	27,500	13.3	2068
9	164,700	242	681	27,450	11.8	1194
10	250,400	462	542	25,040	10.2	1705
11	316,656	440	720	26,388	14.9	1758
12	102,600	242	424	25,650	17.1	975
13	313,524	440	713	29,127	23.5	1238
14	79,218	242	327	26,406	18.8	560

those few racks that could not be measured, the power profile of each piece of equipment was used to estimate the power dissipation.

The CRACs and lighting also contributed to the overall heat load in the data center. Since none of the CRACs had humidification or reheat capabilities, the only power was that for a 10 hp (7457 W) blower. This power was used for all the CRACs, which resulted in a total heat load of 154,700 W. Lighting was provided by fluorescent fixtures rated at 101 W each. With 194 fixtures in this portion of the data center, the resulting total lighting heat load was 19,600 W. Therefore, the total heat load in this portion of the data center was 3.1 MW. The maximum error in this total heat load value was estimated to be ±3%.

Airflow Measurements

The airflow from the perforated floor tiles was measured with a velometer. This flow tool fit exactly over one perforated tile and provided an excellent means of rapidly profiling the flow throughout the data center. Measured flows from each tile or cable cut-out was very stable, varying by less than 10 cfm (0.28 m^3/min).

Measuring the cable cut-out airflows could not be done directly since it was impossible to position the flow tool exactly over the cable cut-out due to cable interference. To eliminate this interference, a short, rectangular, open-ended box with a small cut-out on the side for the cables to enter was installed on the bottom of the instrument. Measurements were made of a select number of cable cut-outs that included all the various sizes distributed throughout the raised-access floor.

The overall flow of the data center was based on all the measurements, the sum of which was 267,305 cfm (7569 m^3/min) (after adjusting for the calibration in the flowmeter). Two additional areas of flow not accounted for are the leakage of air that occurs between the perforated tiles and the leakage through openings around the perimeter between the subfloor and raised-access floor. Based on an energy balance, this leakage flow could be as high as 20% of the total flow from the CRACs. Attempts to seal the perimeter with cardboard and tape were made, but many cables penetrated the perimeter, allowing for air to escape into other parts of the data center.

Temperature Measurements

Air temperature measurements were made at the perforated floor tiles, at the inlet to the racks at a height of 68.9 in. (1750 mm), and at the inlet to the CRACs. The temperature differences between the raised-access floor exhaust air temperature and the temperature of the air entering the rack at a height of 68.9 in. (50 mm) are shown in Table 2.10. Temperatures were taken in accordance with ASHRAE guidelines (ASHRAE 2004)—2 in. (50 mm) in front of the rack covers.

The measurement point near the top of the rack (1750 mm) was selected for several reasons. Both modeling and experimental data suggest that any hot spots can be captured with measurement of this point near the top of the rack. Recirculation of hot air over the top of the rack will definitely be captured by measuring this point.

Secondly, only one point of measurement was selected in order to minimize the time needed to collect data and still capture key thermal characteristics of the data center.

ANALYSIS AND COMPARISONS

Thermal Profiles

Table 2.10 shows the thermal profile of each region displayed in Figures 2.32 and 2.33. The heat fluxes in each of these regions were very high, ranging from 327–720 W/ft^2 (3520–7750 W/m^2), corresponding to the very high rack powers shown in column 5 of Table 2.10. The average rack heat load varied from approximately 24,000–27,000 W. These rack powers resulted in rack heat densities (based on rack footprint) of approximately 1800–2000 W/ft^2 (19,000–22,000 W/m^2).

In Figure 2.32, regions 2–4 and 6–8 (shown between the vertical dotted lines) have the most racks that exceed the inlet air temperature specification. In these regions, 73% of the racks exceeded the inlet air temperature specification (59°F–90°F or 10°C–32°C for the p575 racks). If one considers that the racks in these regions are cooled by the CRACs adjacent to these regions (CRACs A–D and I–L), then one can perform a simple energy balance to determine if adequate cooling exists. The power dissipated by the racks in these six regions is 382 tons (1,342,000 W), while the air-conditioning capability in this region is only 240 tons (844,000 W)— quite a heat load imbalance. Regions 11–14 and half of region 10 in Figure 2.33 (shown between the vertical dotted lines) displayed similar conditions, where 67% of the racks in these regions exceeded the rack inlet air temperature specifications. The power dissipated by the racks in these regions was 230 tons (809,000 W), while the air-conditioning capability of CRACs P, Q, T, S, W, and V was only 180 tons (633,000 W).

As stated in Schmidt and Iyengar (2005a), gaps between racks that dissipate high heat loads and have high flow rates may cause the hot exhaust air to travel into the next cold aisle and be ingested into those racks. For almost the entire ASC Purple layout in the Poughkeepsie system, there were gaps between the racks that allowed hot air from the exhaust of the racks to blow into the adjacent cold aisle and be ingested into the air inlets of the racks. In order to verify this effect, the racks with gaps between them in region 13 were tested with and without blockages. To create the blockages, foam core sheets were cut to size and placed between each of the racks. Air inlet temperatures of the top nodes in four racks were measured before and after the blockages. These results are displayed in Figure 2.34. Each of the racks showed lower air inlet temperatures by as much as 10.8°F (6°C).

Schmidt (2004) and Schmidt and Iyengar (2005a, 2005b) stated that if the flow rate from tiles directly in front of a rack was one-quarter to one-half (0.25–0.5) of the rack flow rate, and the underfloor exhaust air temperature was 59°F (15°C) or less, then conditions would support the manufacturers' air temperature specification. From a review of all the regions reported in this study, the tile flow rates did fall within this range and, in many cases, the underfloor exhaust temperature was 59°F (15°C)

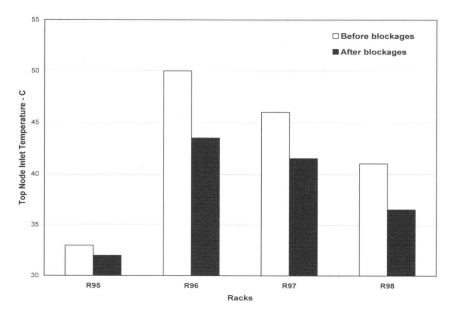

Figure 2.34 Impact of blockages placed between openings in adjacent racks—before and after temperature data.

or below, but the rack inlet air temperature was not within the temperature specification of 50°F–89.6°F (10°C–32°C). The two reasons for regions exceeding rack temperature specifications, even though the perforated tile flow rate appeared to be adequate, were that the heat load capabilities of the nearby CRACs were not sufficient, and gaps existed between racks, allowing hot air to infiltrate into the cold aisle.

The regions (1,5,9, and half of region 10 adjacent to region 9) have racks that are mostly within the rack temperature specifications. What can be said about these regions as opposed to those that exceed rack temperature specifications is that these regions have adequate CRAC cooling capacity. That is not true for the other regions.

SUMMARY

Based on the test results of the ASC Purple cluster in the IBM data center, the following can be considered as necessary and sufficient conditions for achieving rack inlet air temperature within specifications:

1. The perforated tiles immediately in front of a rack must exhaust a minimum of one-quarter to one-half (0.25–0.5) of the rack airflow rate with a chilled-air temperature below 59°F (15°C).

2. The air-conditioning capability must meet or exceed the requirements of nearby racks being cooled.
3. Gaps between high-powered racks should be closed off to avoid the hot exhaust air being blown into the next cold aisle.

REFERENCES

ASHRAE. 2004. *Thermal Guidelines for Data Processing Environments.* Atlanta: American Society of Heating, Refrigerating and Air-Conditioning Engineers, Inc.

Schmidt, R.R. 2004. Thermal profile of a high density data center—Methodology to thermally characterize a data center. *ASHRAE Transactions* 110(2):635–42.

Schmidt, R.R., and M. Iyengar. 2005a. Effect of data center layout on rack inlet air temperatures. *Proceedings of InterPACK 2005, San Francisco, California.*

Schmidt, R.R., and M. Iyengar. 2005b. Thermal profile of a high density data center. *ASHRAE Transactions* 111(2):765–77.

2.2   RAISED-ACCESS FLOOR WITH AHUs ON SUBFLOOR

2.2.1   CASE STUDY 5—LAWRENCE LIVERMORE NATIONAL LAB DATA CENTER

This case study reports the results of thermal profile testing of IBM's ASC Purple, installed at Lawrence Livermore National Lab (see case study 4 for thermal profile results for the Poughkeepsie installation). Those areas of the cluster in Poughkeepsie that did not meet the temperature criteria were well within the temperature limits at the Livermore installation. Based on the results from these two data centers, necessary and sufficient criteria are outlined for IT racks to achieve inlet air temperatures that meet the manufacturers' temperature specifications.

LAYOUT OF DATA CENTER

After ASC Purple was tested in the Poughkeepsie facility and all components were verified as working properly to the customer's specifications, the cluster of racks was disassembled, packed, and shipped to Lawrence Livermore National Labs in Livermore, California, where it was reassembled. The layout of the data center is shown in Figure 2.35. Once the cluster was installed, approximately half the data center was populated with IT equipment, as shown in the figure. The computer room is 126 × 193 ft (38.4 × 58.8 m) and the ASC Purple cluster occupied a space 84 × 88 ft (25.6 × 26.8 m). The computer room has a capability of supporting 7.5 MW of IT equipment, while the ASC Purple system generates approximately 3.2 MW (max of 1280 nodes operating) of electrical load when fully powered (not all the racks were powered in the Poughkeepsie lab because of power/temperature constraints). The racks were arranged in cold-aisle/hot-aisle formation, as shown in the figure, and installed on a raised-access floor. The IT equipment is installed on the second floor of a two-story data center. The lower level is 15 ft high and all the air-handling equipment is installed in this area, as shown in Figure 2.36. This area is slightly pressurized and supplies air through multiple openings at the top of the floor. Directly above these large (10 × 16 ft or 3.05 × 4.9 m) multiple openings is a traditional raised-access floor, 4 ft high, where air is distributed to the perforated tiles arranged throughout the data center. The chilled air is distributed to the perforated tiles, and the hot exhaust air is then returned to the AHUs through openings in the ceiling and in the side walls. The height of the ceiling in the computer room is 10 ft (3.05 m). There were three types of perforated tiles—25% open, 56% open with dampers, and 56% open without dampers. The general airflow path in the data center is depicted in Figure 2.36, along with a picture of the mechanical utility room and a picture of ASC Purple installed on the raised-access floor.

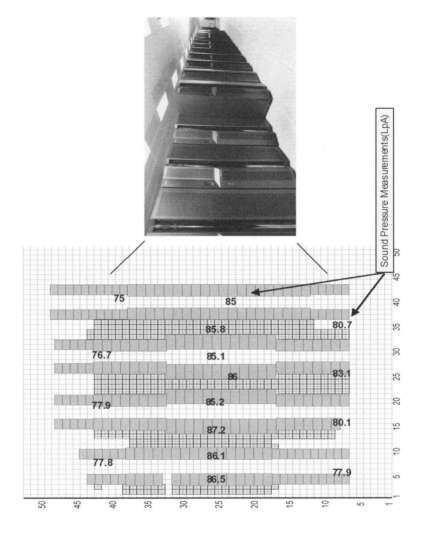

Figure 2.35 Livermore data center—ASC Purple layout.

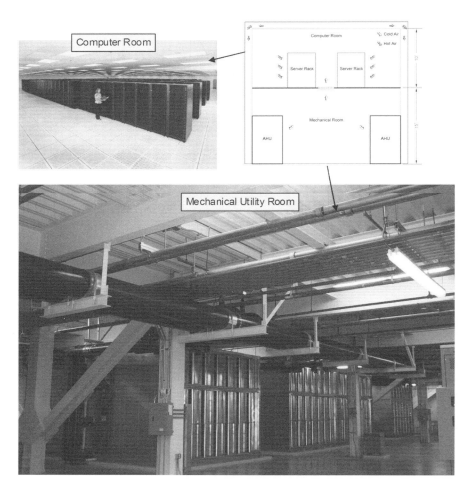

Figure 2.36 Livermore data center airflow path.

MEASUREMENT TOOLS

A flow measurement tool similar to that used at the Poughkeepsie data center (case study 4) was used at Livermore. The tool included calibration features, so no adjustments were needed to correct the measured results.

The temperatures were measured with a handheld thermocouple meter using a type T thermocouple. Since temperature differences and not absolute temperatures were of most importance, the meter was not calibrated, although the error in the thermocouple and instrument was estimated to be ±1.8°F (±1.0°C). Temperature difference errors were estimated to be ±1.8°F (±1.0°C), resulting primarily from cycling of the CRACs.

MEASUREMENT AND RESULTS

Time constraints prevented a full set of measurements from being included in this study, but it is instructive to review some of the key measurements and contrast the results from the Livermore site with those of the same cluster (at reduced power) at the Poughkeepsie development lab (see case study 4). The Livermore site layout is much different from that of the Poughkeepsie site; however, the areas with high heat flux are still very similar. A number of tests were performed for the same applications running on the equipment. During these runs, a number of optimization efforts were performed where the perforated tiles were rearranged and the number of operating AHUs were changed. The data reported in Figures 2.37–2.38 are the results for the layout before and after all the modifications were made in perforated floor tiles and AHUs.

The objectives for this data center were to maintain inlet temperatures for all IT racks at or below 77°F (25°C) (the ASHRAE [2004] recommended temperature specification) and minimizing the number of operating AHUs, thereby reducing energy consumption. As seen in Figure 2.37, the initial temperature results showed 28 racks exceeded 77°F (25°C) inlet air temperature, measured at a height of 5.74 ft (1750 mm) from the raised-access floor and 1.97 in. (50 mm) in front of the rack. Five racks had air temperatures that were 86°F (30°C) or more. The exhaust chilled-air temperature from the raised-access floor was fairly uniform at 55.4°F (13°C). One of the objectives was to reduce all the rack inlet air temperatures to 77°F (25°C) or below. After many iterations of rearranging floor tiles, installing more open floor tiles in those areas that had higher rack inlet air temperatures, and changing the number of AHUs, the final results are shown in Figure 2.37. As seen, only three racks had inlet air temperature above 77°F (25°C)— one rack at 79°F (26°C) and two racks at 80.6°F (27°C). Not only were the inlet air temperatures of most of the racks below 77°F (25°C), two AHUs could be powered off, thereby reducing energy costs. Each AHU delivered 80,000 cfm (2265 m³/min) with a rating of 145 tons (509,820 W). With the fan rated at 75 hp (55,928 W or 55.928 kW), the estimated energy savings of turning two units off is $55,000/yr (at the Livermore Lab electricity rate of $0.056/kWh).

In reviewing Figure 2.37, there are a number of racks that fall below the minimum temperature (68°F [20°C]) recommended by ASHRAE (2004). If inlet air temperatures were measured for the nodes located lower in the rack, most of the data would probably have been nearer to the chilled-air temperature of 55.4°F (13°C) exiting the perforated tiles. Even though the recommended range of air inlet temperature is 68°F–77°F (20°C–25°C), the recommended low temperature value (68°F [20°C]) was adopted by ASHRAE because of energy concerns and not due to the reliability of the IT equipment. The upper recommended limit (77°F [25°C]) was set for IT equipment reliability. The concern was that if a temperature lower than 68°F (20°C)

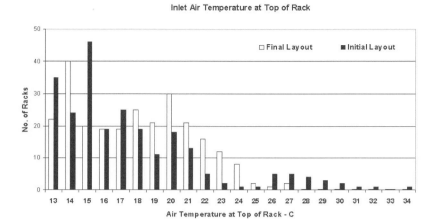

Figure 2.37 Livermore ASC Purple cluster rack inlet temperatures.

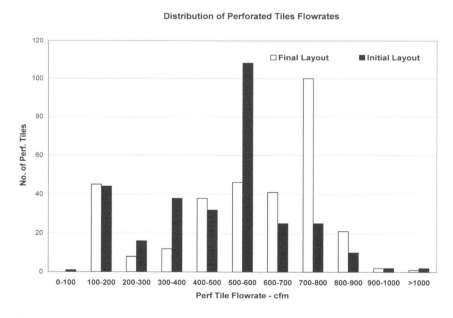

Figure 2.38 Livermore data center ASC Purple perforated tile flow.

was chosen, then facility operators would push their chilled-air temperatures even lower, thereby wasting energy and not really improving IT equipment reliability.

Although measurements of flows from all the perforated tiles were not possible, measurements were taken for as many perforated tiles as time allowed. The perforated tile locations for ASC Purple's area are shown in Figure 2.35. All the perforated tiles directly in front of the racks were measured. Those in the middle or at the ends of rows were not measured. The perforated tile flow rates for the initial and final layouts are shown in Figure 2.38. Although the tile layout remained almost the same, the perforated tile openings were modified. Some 25% open tiles were replaced with 56% open tiles with dampers, and some tiles with dampers were removed to provide even higher flows. In reviewing Figure 2.38, more tiles had flow at the upper range for the final layout, even though two AHUs were turned off, which indicates that the floor provided a high impedance to the flow, and opening up the tiles allowed more flow through. The total flow through the tiles measured in the initial layout was 145,000 cfm (4,106 m³/min), while in the final layout it was 177,000 cfm (5,012 m³/min). More of the air was directed where it was needed, even though the total flow from the AHUs decreased. Obviously the flow from the perforated tiles measured is much less than the total flow delivered by the operating AHUs. Airflow from the AHUs passes through cable openings, cracks between tiles, and to areas of another data center space with IT equipment and associated perforated tiles.

The airflow from the perforated tiles in front of the p575 racks was examined, and the average of all these flows was 690 cfm (19.5 m³/min). However, the tiles in front of the p575 racks took up an area of more than one tile. In most of the areas measured, the middle tile in the cold aisle, which was three tiles wide, also contributed to the air ingested into the rack. Taking this middle tile into consideration, the total flow at the front of the p575 rack was approximately 1290 cfm (36.5 m³/min). As in prior measurements of data centers, a rule of thumb was established for what amount of flow was required from a floor tile compared to the flow through a rack. The nominal flow through the rack was approximately 2800 cfm (79.3 m³/min). The flow through the tiles immediately in front of the rack (1290 cfm or 36.5 m³/min) was slightly less than half the flow through the rack (2800 cfm or 79.3 m³/min), which again confirmed this rule of thumb. The remaining flow is provided elsewhere in the data center through the mixing of hot and cold air from cable openings, leakage from the small cracks between tiles, etc.

Examination of the Livermore data center finds good agreement with the criteria established in case study 4 for how to achieve rack inlet temperatures within the air temperature inlet specification:

1. The flow rate from the tiles in front of the racks falls within the range of one-quarter to one-half (0.25–0.5) the flow rate through the rack.
2. The exhaust chilled-air temperature is below 59°F (15°C).
3. The air-conditioning capability is more than adequate given the heat load. The eight operating AHUs (final state after the optimization of the raised-access floor) had a combined capacity of 1160 tons (4,079,000 W), while the power

dissipated by the IT equipment was approximately 810 tons (2,848,000 W) (1200 nodes operating, with 1280 nodes max operating nodes).

4. No gaps existed between the racks to allow for hot air exhausting into the next cold aisle to disturb the hot-aisle/cold-aisle arrangement.

Finally, measurements were taken of the acoustical levels within the data center. The measurements were taken with a Quest Technologies Noise Pro series DLX dosimeter. Sound pressure levels were measured and are shown in the layout of Figure 2.35. In the middle of the rows, the sound pressure levels ranged from 85–87.1 dB, while on the ends of the rows they ranged from 75–83.1 dB. The AHUs located in the mechanical utility room on the lower level displayed values of 72–74.5 dB. If the sound pressure levels exceed 90 dB, then hearing protection is required (USDOL 2006). Similar requirements are enforced by the European Union (ERA 2003).

SUMMARY

From the results of both the Livermore production environment and the Poughkeepsie test environment (see case study 4), a clearer picture evolves of the conditions necessary to ensure that the rack inlet temperature will meet the manufacturers temperature conditions. Based on prior studies (Schmidt 2004; Schmidt and Iyengar 2005a, 2005b) and the results at Livermore, it is necessary that the flow exiting the floor tiles in front of the rack be one-quarter to one-half (0.25–0.5) of the rack flow rate at a supply temperature of 59°F (15°C) or less in order to meet the inlet air temperature for the rack. However, as the results on the test floor in Poughkeepsie indicate, these are not the only required conditions. Even though the one-quarter to one-half rule was met in Poughkeepsie and the supply chilled-air temperature was less than 59°F (15°C) in most cases, many rack inlet air temperatures were much higher than the rack specification. Two conditions existed that contributed to these rack inlet air temperatures exceeding specifications. One was the gaps between the racks that allowed high-velocity hot exhaust air to be blown into the cold aisles, upsetting the cold-aisle/hot-aisle arrangement. The second was that the CRACs in the region of the high-powered racks were not sufficient to handle the high heat load. Based on these two data centers' results and the results of Schmidt (2004) and Schmidt and Iyengar (2005a, 2005b), the necessary and sufficient conditions required to maintain the inlet air temperature into a rack within the manufacturers' specifications are four-fold:

1. One-quarter to one-half (0.25–0.5) of the rack flow rate exhausting from the perforated tiles directly in front of the rack
2. Supply chilled-air temperature below 59° (15°C) (or higher if the chilled-air exhausting from the tiles is higher)
3. No gaps between racks that allow high-powered/high-flow hot exhaust air to be blown into the next cold aisle
4. Equal or greater air-conditioning capability in the region of the high-powered racks

This case study describes a specific set of measurements from a high density data center in order to provide details of the thermal profile. In addition, the data collection techniques described can be used as a basis for collecting data from other data centers or telecom rooms and provide a presentation format in which to display the information.

REFERENCES

ASHRAE. 2004. *Thermal Guidelines for Data Processing Environments.* Atlanta: American Society of Heating, Refrigerating and Air-Conditioning Engineers, Inc.

ERA. 2003. European workplace noise directive. Directive 2003/10/EC, European Rotogravure Association, Munich, Germany.

Schmidt, R.R. 2004. Thermal profile of a high density data center—Methodology to thermally characterize a data center. *ASHRAE Transactions* 110(2):635–42.

Schmidt, R.R., and M. Iyengar. 2005a. Effect of data center layout on rack inlet air temperatures. *Proceedings of InterPACK 2005, San Francisco, California.*

Schmidt, R.R., and M. Iyengar. 2005b. Thermal profile of a high density data center. *ASHRAE Transactions* 111(2):765–77.

USDOL. 2006. Occupational noise exposure. Hearing Conservation Standard 29 CFR 1910.95, United States Department of Labor, Occupational Safety and Health Administration, Washington, DC.

2.3   RAISED-ACCESS FLOOR SUPPLY/CEILING RETURN

2.3.1   CASE STUDY 6—NYC FINANCIAL SERVICES DATA CENTER

All data centers are designed to an average heat density expressed in W/ft^2. This represents the total power dissipated in the room compared to the total size of the space. In practice, data centers are not populated according to this average heat density but are actually pockets of various heat densities above and below the average. The data center cooling system is designed for the average heat density but has the ability to cool areas of the data center at levels higher than average. Understanding how the air-conditioning system performs gives the data center operator the opportunity to coordinate placement of the highest-power hardware loads in areas where maximum cooling can be achieved. This case study looks at a data center where the hardware placement was coordinated so that the highest power loads were placed where the highest static pressure in the raised-access floor was expected. The cooling design is a raised-access floor supply with a ceiling plenum return.

This case study describes the thermal performance of a 4770 ft^2 (445 m^2) data center that measures approximately 53 × 90 ft (16.2 × 27.5 m). The data center houses a variety of servers from small rack-mounted servers to large stand-alone partitioned servers and blade servers. The space includes the network cable frame and storage area network (SAN) infrastructure required for the production applications residing on the servers. The space, formerly a tape library, was converted to a data center in 2003. The load has grown from an initial level of 45 W/ft^2 (481 W/m^2) to the current level of 105 W/ft^2 (1123 W/m^2). The heat density in the room is not uniform; some cabinet loads are less than 2 kW, while some large servers exceed 20 kW. More details are given later in the "Measurement and Results" section.

To quantify the thermal performance of the data center, temperature measurements were taken at various locations. Most important, readings were taken at the hardware inlet as recommended in *Thermal Guidelines for Data Processing Environments* (ASHRAE 2004). In addition, supply and return air temperature and airflow measurements were recorded.

LAYOUT OF THE DATA CENTER

The data center profiled is a financial services data center located in New York City. All equipment is located on the raised-access floor in an enclosed area measuring approximately 53 × 90 ft (16.2 × 27.5 m). A plan view of the data center is included in Figure 2.39.

The data center space of interest is isolated from surrounding data center spaces. Perimeter walls are constructed from slab to slab. The space contains 84 server cabinets, 11 network cable frames, and 24 freestanding large servers. The network frames are used primarily for cabling, with switches located in some of the server cabinets close to the frames. The frames are positioned directly in front of two

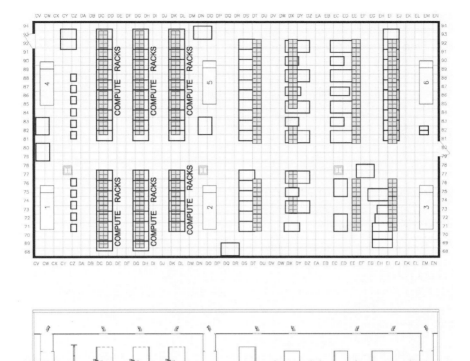

Figure 2.39 Layout of data center.

CRACs in an area expected to have low static pressure. The design intent was to position the low heat density equipment where the low static pressure was expected and the high heat density equipment where the highest static pressure was expected. The cabinets are installed in a traditional hot-aisle/cold-aisle arrangement with a front-to-front and back-to-back placement. The computer room air-handling units (CRAHs) are arranged parallel to the server cabinets and the rows of freestanding hardware. All CRAHs are down-flow type, supplying air to a 24 in. plenum, and are ducted directly to the ceiling for the return air path. The depth of the ceiling plenum is approximately 5 ft. Two units are placed against the wall at the west end of the data center, two more units are placed approximately 34 ft away facing the same direction, and two more units are placed an additional 46 ft away at the east end of the data center facing the direction opposite the other four units. The total of six CRAHs includes one for redundancy. The electrical equipment in the data center consists of eight PDUs and two remote power panels (RPPs). The RPPs are fed from the PDUs and are required to provide additional circuit positions. Control panels for pre-action sprinklers, a smoke-detection system, and building management system (BMS) monitoring are located on the perimeter walls. Lighting is pendant hung, which minimizes the impact to the ceiling grid and is coordinated with the hardware layout. The ceiling consists of standard tiles and return-air grilles. The position of the return-air grilles can be changed to accommodate changing heat loads.

MEASUREMENT TOOLS

The instruments in Table 2.11 were used to record data in this case study.

MEASUREMENT AND RESULTS

Power Measurements

Measurements of the input power to the data center were made at several levels to provide an accurate representation of the power of the various types of equipment distributed throughout the space. The power to all the hardware is provided through eight PDUs located in the room. Each PDU has a digital display indicating the current, voltage, and power in kW. These readings are listed in the attached Table 2.12. The total power provided by the PDUs is 504 kW.

The server cabinets each have two three-phase power strips to provide power to the servers. Each power strip is connected to a different uninterruptable power supply (UPS) source, providing a redundant supply for all dual cord loads. The power strips also have digital displays of the current on each phase. A survey of the power strips provides the load in each of the cabinets (see Table 2.13). The cabinets are separated into north and south groups for this analysis, corresponding to their relationship to the air-conditioning placement. The loads range from 1.7–5.52 kW per cabinet. Table 2.14 lists the loads in each of the 84 cabinets.

The freestanding servers and blades do not have digital displays of the power used by each device. Individual circuit measurements were taken by using a Fluke Mutimeter 87-3 at the PDUs and RPPs. The freestanding devices are also grouped

Table 2.11   Measurement Tools

Function	Manufacturer	Model/Device	Model #
Temperature gun	Raytek	Raynger ST	RAYST8LXU
Temperature sensor	Cooper Industries	Electro thermometer	SH66A
Velometer	Pacer Industries	Digital thermometer anemometer datalogger	DTA4000
Static pressure	Shortridge Industries	Air data multimeter	ADM-870
PDU current	Fluke	Multimeter	87-3

Table 2.12   PDU Measurements

PDU	kVA Rating	Actual Power Reading, kW
7E15 (1)	150	57
7E15 (1)	150	57
7E14 (6)	150	57
7D2 (5)	150	63
7E13 (6)	150	71
7E16 (1)	150	59
7D1 (5)	150	70
7D3 (5)	150	61
7E18 (6)	150	66
Power Consumed, kW		**504**
Occupied Area, ft^2		4773
Power Density, W/ft^2		**105.59**

Table 2.13   Cabinet Power Loads

Cabinet	Density, kW	Cabinet	Density, kW	Cabinet	Density, kW
CZ91	3.6	DC91	5.52	DG91	3.60
CZ90	4.8	DC90	2.52	DG90	2.88
		DC89	N/A	DG89	4.08
		DC88	1.80	DG88	2.76
		DC87	1.92	DG87	2.88
		DC86	1.92	DG86	3.48
		DC85	N/A	DG85	4.32
		DC84	N/A	DG84	3.96
		DC83	1.92	DG83	3.48
		DC82	1.92	DG82	3.00
		DC81	2.16	DG81	3.24
		DC77	2.28	DG77	2.64
		DC76	2.04	DG76	1.68
		DC75	2.04	DG75	2.88
		DC74	3.96	DG74	3.72
		DC73	4.20	DG73	2.16
		DC72	3.48	DG72	1.80
		DC71	N/A	DG71	3.96
		DC70	N/A	DG70	N/A

Table 2.14   Cabinet Power Loads

Cabinet	Density, kW	Cabinet	Density, kW	Cabinet	Density, kW
DK91	2.04	—	—	EI91	3.30
DK90	3.60	DS90	2.64	EI90	5.40
DK89	2.88	DS89	2.52	EI89	5.00
DK88	1.56	DS88	2.76	EI88	4.60
DK87	4.32	DS87	3.84	EI87	5.30
DK86	2.88	DS86	2.76	EI86	4.50
DK85	2.64	DS85	2.76	EI85	2.70
DK84	3.96	DS84	2.88	EI84	3.50
DK83	3.00	DS83	2.04	EI83	3.00
DK82	4.56	DS82	2.40	EI82	3.00
DK81	3.84	DS81	2.16	EI81	4.20
DK77	2.76	DS77	3.60		
DK76	3.12	DS76	1.68		
DK75	4.32	DS75	2.16		
DK74	4.32	DS74	1.68		
DK73	2.04	DS73	2.40		
DK72	4.08	DS72	2.40		

as north and south for this analysis. The loads range from 2.0–23.1 kW. Table 2.15 lists the loads of the freestanding devices.

The server cabinets employ fans in the top to assist in removing heat from the servers and discharge it vertically toward the ceiling return plenum. The power for the fans is supplied by the power strips in the cabinets; therefore, it is included in the total power indicated for each cabinet. The fans are variable speed with the control determined by a preselected and adjustable discharge temperature. The power draw for each fan is 0.5 amps at full speed. The maximum power used for fans in each cabinet is 0.35 kW.

The total power read at the devices and at the power strips in the server cabinets was 483.6 kW, or 95.9% of the power readings at the PDUs. Figure 2.40 illustrates the total power in each row of equipment.

Airflow Measurements

Airflow was measured at the CRAHs and around the data center space. In addition, static pressure was measured across the data center floor to confirm the design intent of locating the lowest loads in the area of lowest static pressure and the highest loads in the area of highest static pressure.

Table 2.15   Freestanding Servers/Blades Power Measurements

Device	Density, kW	Device	Density, kW	Device	Density, kW
DY91	12.6	ED91	21.3	EH74	19.7
DY90	1.8	ED90	2.7	EH73	2.0
DY88	21.8	ED88	10.5	EI73	5.9
DY86	2.3	ED86	2.9	EI72	0.0
DY84	22.3	ED84	13.2	EI71	6.0
DY83	2.4	ED83	0.4	EI70	7.2
DY81	21.4	ED81	11.4		
DY76	23.1				
DY75	2.3				
DY74	23.1				
DY72	3.6				

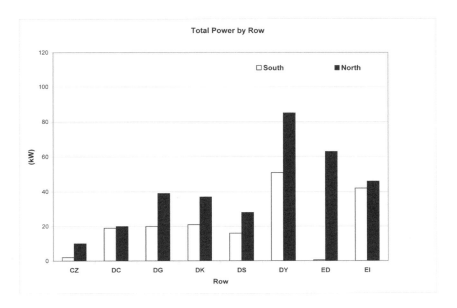

Figure 2.40 IT power by row—north/south.

Airflow in the data center begins with the CRAH. In this case, the supply air is discharged directly into the raised-access floor plenum from the downflow design of the CRAHs. The actual airflow was measured at 105,000 cfm and compared to the published specification for the units. Table 2.16 lists the results.

The cooling air leaves the underfloor plenum one of two ways: through controlled openings and through uncontrolled openings. In this data center, the controlled openings are the bases of the server cabinets with the adjustable grommets and the high volume perforated tiles in the areas of the freestanding servers. The uncontrolled openings include cable openings at the hardware, power cable openings under PDUs, and leakage around raised-access floor tiles.

The supply of air through the controlled openings is dependent on the static pressure present. Static pressure was measured across the data center floor in a grid pattern, and the results are shown in Figure 2.41.

Table 2.16   CRAH Airflow Rate

CRAC Unit Airflow	
Specified	Measured
19,000 CFM	17,500 CFM

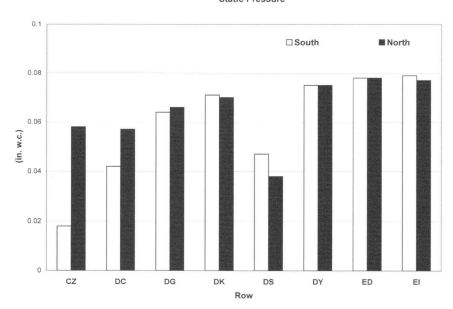

Figure 2.41 Underfloor static pressure—north/south.

With the static pressure known, the flow through the controlled openings was predictable.

Performance curves for the high volumetric airflow perforated tiles used near the large freestanding servers showed an expected volume of 945 cfm (26.8 m^3/min) for each tile for the range of static pressure present.

The adjustable grommets in the bases of the server cabinets were tested at various opening positions and various static pressures by the cabinet manufacturer. The results showed an average plenum supply volumetric airflow of 540 cfm (15.3 m^3/min) in each cabinet at the static pressures present in this data center.

The total airflow through all controlled openings was then calculated by adding up all the high volume perforated tiles and all the cabinet base openings. The results showed a total controlled volume of 81,286 cfm (2301.8 m^3/min) compared to a total supplied volume of 105,000 cfm (2932.2 m^3/min); 77.4% of the cooling was delivered through controlled openings, and 22.6% entered the space through other means.

Airflow through the server cabinets is produced by the six fans on top. Each fan is rated for 225 cfm (6.4 m^3/min) at full speed, or 1350 cfm (38.2 m^3/min) total for the cabinet. The total flow into the cabinet is, therefore, a combination of the cooling air from the raised-access floor plenum supplied through the grommets in the cabinet base and the room air pulled into the cabinet through the openings in the front and rear doors. When the fans run at full speed this results in 540 cfm (15.3 m^3/min) of plenum air mixed with 810 cfm (22.9 m^3/min) of room air. The air entering through the front door of the cabinet raises the temperature of the plenum air to produce a hardware-entering temperature in the recommended range, and the air entering through the rear door lowers the hardware discharge temperature before it is exhausted from the cabinet. The volume of air entering through the cabinet doors varies as the speed of the cabinet fans changes to maintain the discharge air setpoint. The amount of plenum air entering through the cabinet base can be reduced by closing the adjustable grommets.

All return air flows back to the CRAHs through the ceiling grilles positioned over the hardware. To verify that the return air is balanced, airflow measurements were taken at the return grilles (see Figure 2.42). The results showed that there were no areas of low velocity or no flow. The presence of good velocity across all the return grille areas is an indication that the hot discharge air is being returned to the CRAHs without recirculation to the cabinet or large server intakes. The lowest return air volume was measured in an area directly above three PDUs. If the data center operator wanted to change the distribution of the return air within the space, the ceiling grilles could be repositioned.

Temperature Measurements

The most important temperature in a data center is the air inlet temperature to the hardware. This confirms that adequate cooling is being provided according to ASHRAE recommendations (ASHRAE 2004). The second most important temperature in the data center is the return air temperature to the CRAHs.

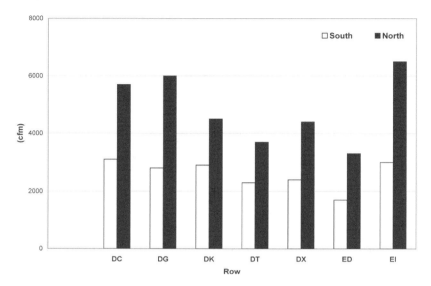

Figure 2.42 Return airflow rate—north/south.

This confirms that adequate cooling can continue to be provided to the computer hardware.

In this case study, temperatures were measured at the inlet to hardware in a representative number of cabinets and freestanding devices in each row. The readings were taken at the bottom, middle, and top of the hardware elevation, except where freestanding devices drew supply air only from the bottom or lower elevation. The locations were selected at the ends and middle of each row. The readings are grouped into north and south sides of the data center in Figures 2.43–2.44. Temperatures were also recorded at the return to the CRAHs, as shown in Figure 2.45.

THERMAL PERFORMANCE AND ANALYSIS

Heat Densities

This data center exhibited a wide range of heat densities across a relatively small area. The server cabinets contained loads ranging form 1.7–5.52 kW. Based on the cabinet footprint, this produced a heat density range of 208–675 W/ft^2. The freestanding devices produced a wide range of loads from 2.0–23.1 kW in a single enclosure. Based on the footprint of the device, this resulted in a maximum power density of 1604 W/ft^2.

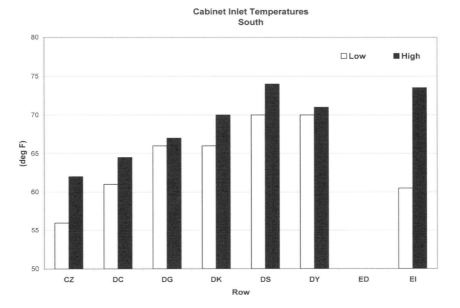

Figure 2.43 Cabinet inlet air temperatures—south.

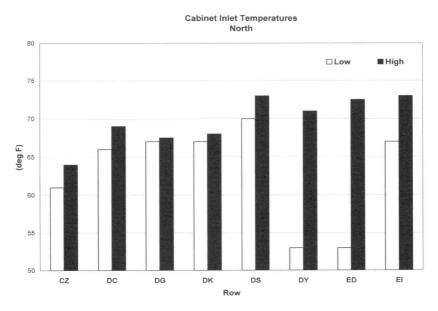

Figure 2.44 Cabinet inlet air temperatures—north.

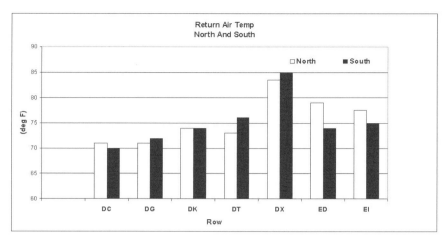

Figure 2.45 CRAH return air temperatures—north/south.

The power density across the room is not evenly distributed. The east end of the room containing the freestanding large servers, blades, and some cabinets occupies 40% of the space but consumes 60% of the power. This produces a heat flux of 150 W/ft^2 (1600 W/m^2). The west end of the room containing the majority of the server cabinets and network frames occupies 60% of the space but consumes 40% of the power. This produces a heat flux of 73.2 W/ft^2 (788 W/m^2).

The overall room area of 4770 ft^2 (443 m^2) with the total PDU load of 504 kW resulted in an average density of 105.6 W/ft^2 (1136.7 W/m^2).

Temperatures

The air temperature leaving the server cabinets is controlled at each cabinet by a setpoint that controls the speed of the fans on top of the cabinets. Most of the cabinets in this data center maintain a discharge temperature of 81°F (27.2°C). The large free-standing devices exhibited higher discharge temperatures, with most in the 88°F–95°F range (31.1°C–35°C). However, one blade cabinet had a discharge temperature of 112.2°F (45.5°C).

For the server cabinets, comparing the graphs of the inlet temperatures (Figures 2.43–2.44) to the cabinet discharge temperatures (Figure 2.45) shows a difference of less than 20°F (11°C). This results from tempering the hardware discharge temperature with room air brought in through the rear door.

For the free-standing devices, comparing the graphs of the inlet temperatures to the discharge temperatures shows a difference of over 40°F (22.2°C). Despite the high discharge temperatures, the return air temperatures measured at the ceiling return grilles were below 80°F (26.7°C), with the exception of the grilles above column line DX of Figure 2.39, where it reached 83°F (28.3°C). In all cases, supply air from the raised-access floor entering the room through uncontrolled openings mixed with the discharge air from both the cabinets and the free-standing devices to produce a return temperature well within the capacity of the CRAHs.

The server inlet temperatures were recorded at the ends and middle of each cabinet row and at the ends and middle of each row of free-standing devices. In almost all cases, the low readings were slightly below the range recommended by ASHRAE (2004), and the high readings were well below the high limit. This indicates that adjustments can be made to raise these temperatures. In the case of the server cabinets, the grommet openings can be reduced to introduce less supply air from the raised-access floor to each cabinet. In the case of the free-standing devices, the adjustable perforated tiles can be closed down incrementally to supply less cold air to the server intake. If necessary, the supply air temperature can be raised also.

Static Pressure

The static pressure survey confirmed that the area of highest static pressure was at the east end of the data center. This corresponded to the area of highest installed power load. With this information, the data center operator can feel confident in being able to cool power densities higher than the average design of the room. The static pressure increases from the west end of the room to the east end of the room, with a slight dip in front of the CRAHs in the middle of the room. This is the result of the increase in velocity directly in front of the middle units. The lowest static pressure was measured at the west end of the room near the CRAHs and near the low power density network cable frames. The static pressure readings at the west end were not consistent from the north side to the south side. Upon inspection of the underfloor plenum, it was discovered that a large concentration of network cable existed directly downstream from the north CRAH. This produced blockage sufficient to cause the unexpected high static pressure in column line CZ of Figure 2.39.

In general, the static pressure in the data center is quite high. This is the result of all CRAHs operating, including the redundant unit. A further study would survey the static pressure across the floor in six different modes, with each CRAH in the OFF position. This would allow the operator to know if the data center cooling is sufficient in all redundant modes.

Return Temperature

The graphs of the return air temperatures show an increase from the west end of the room to the east end of the room. This follows the profile of the increasing power at the east end of the room. With the return air temperatures well within the range of the CRAHs, this is a perfectly acceptable situation. If the power density increases further at the east end of the room, the high static pressure at that end would allow the data center operator to introduce more cooling air from the raised-access floor to maintain the return air temperatures in an acceptable range.

The survey of hardware inlet temperatures showed no elevated temperatures at the ends of the cabinet rows. The ceiling return design appears to prevent recirculation of hot exhaust air to the inlet of the servers.

ENERGY BALANCE

To confirm the accuracy of the data presented, via an energy balance, a calculation of airflow using measured power input and temperature difference is compared to the actual airflow calculated to see if they match. The overall data center airflow through the cabinet bases, the high-volume perforated tiles, and cable openings was calculated to be 97,641 cfm (2765 m³/min). Using the CRAH average temperature difference (52.8°F [11.6°C] supply; 72.8°F [22.7°C] return) and the overall heat load for the space (504 kW), the expected airflow is 92,888 cfm (2630 m³/min). This is within 4.9% of the calculated value. Both of these values are less than the measured airflow taken at the CRAH returns of 105,000 cfm (2973 m³/min). Upon inspection of the underfloor condition, some openings were observed in the perimeter wall. Although measurements were not taken, the size and presence of these openings could account for the 7359 cfm (208 m³/min) difference between the calculated value and that measured at the CRAHs.

SUMMARY

This case study provides a review of a high density data center with a cooling design using a raised-access floor supply plenum and a return air ceiling plenum. The study makes use of information available to most data center operators, including detailed power and temperature readings at the cabinet and device level, static pressure measurements, and airflow readings. By understanding where the highest cooling capacity will be in a data center, the operator can design his or her hardware layout to take advantage of high density installations.

2.4 RAISED-ACCESS FLOOR WITH HEAT EXCHANGERS ADJACENT TO SERVER RACKS

2.4.1 CASE STUDY 7—GEORGIA INSTITUTE OF TECHNOLOGY DATA CENTER

The case study of the Georgia Institute of Technology Razor HPC cluster at the Center for the Study of Systems Biology demonstrates a solution for two parametric challenges: space utilization and cooling. A water-cooled, rack-level heat exchanger was deployed to help create a very high density ($300W/ft^2$ [3.2 kW/m^2]) cooling solution within an existing facility where significant cooling limitations existed. In effect, the RDHx solution allowed for the creation of an area with cooling density ten times greater than the capabilities of the rest of the facility.

LAYOUT OF DATA CENTER

It was established by the end user that the computing cluster would initially consist primarily of 1000 blade servers. In addition, support configurations of storage, management, and networking hardware were required to operate Razor. Table 2.17 provides a summary of the power and cooling requirements for the computer cluster.

The original floor plan layout considered for the facility, requiring approximately 1600 ft^2 (149 m^2), is shown in Figure 2.46. The layout shows fully loaded racks of blades (6 chassis per rack) in the 12 interior racks. Support infrastructure is depicted by the corner racks in Figure 2.46. An alternate method for deploying the blades across this square footage is to populate each rack half way (3 chassis per rack), with twice as many interior racks. These additional racks would reside in the open spaces between the existing racks.

A number of user-imposed challenges forced formulation of a more nimble implementation plan. First, the hosting environment for the cluster was required to be of showcase quality; aesthetics were of the utmost importance. The area was intended to accommodate tours, and large areas of underutilized floor space were deemed undesirable, so the floor area of the cluster was required to be reduced to a bare minimum. Excessive noise and discomfort from air movement were likewise

Table 2.17   Planned Cooling Requirements

Equipment	# of Racks	Rack Power, kW	Total Power, kW	Cooling Tons
Blades	12	23.2	278.0	79
Storage	2	4.9	9.8	2.8
Management	1	5.0	5.0	1.4
Networking	1	6.2	6.2	1.8
		Total	**299.0**	**85.0**

required to be reduced to a minimum. Finally, an extremely tight schedule for design and build required that the facility be completed in roughly 30 days.

In order to meet the requirements of the mounting challenges, the strategic decision to employ a rear-door heat exchanger (RDHX) was made. The device is a copper-tube, aluminum-fin, air-to-water heat exchanger that replaces the rear panel of a computer rack. Hot air from the server exhausts passes across the heat exchanger coil, which removes at least 55% to 60% of the rack heat load from the airstream before it enters the room. The system is completely open with no supplemental air movers required. Water is circulated through the heat exchangers by a remote pumping unit that includes a water-to-water heat exchanger by which heat is rejected to an on-site chilled-water system (the primary loop). The technology cooling system loop (secondary loop) delivers conditioned water to the RDHXs at a flow rate of 7 to 10 gpm (0.44 to 0.63 L/s), maintained at a temperature of 60°F to 64°F (16°C to 18°C) to avoid condensation. Water-side pressure drop at the design flow rate is approximately 7 psi (48 kPa). The RDHX function significantly reduces the burden on the room air-conditioning system and cuts down on the air-conditioning capacity required. It was decided to implement this technology only on the racks filled with high density blade servers.

The first challenge the heat exchangers resolved was underutilized floor space. By utilizing the heat exchangers, it became possible to fully load six blade chassis per

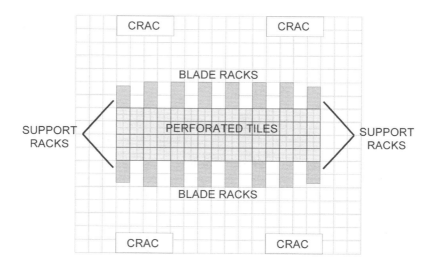

Figure 2.46 Original cooling plan (traditional raised floor cooling; non-high density).

cabinet. In this manner, the square footage required to house and cool the cluster was reduced to an optimal 1000 ft² (93 m²). Removal of such a large amount of heat from the room airstream significantly reduced the amount of air movement necessary for the cooling solution, thereby reducing noise and discomfort and mitigating the second challenge. Finally, the facility had—in surplus—four spare 20 ton (240 kBtu/h) CRACs that could provide exactly the amount of sensible air-side cooling required with N+1 redundancy. This helped alleviate the final concern regarding the implementation schedule. Figure 2.47 shows the final floor layout, which requires only about 1000 ft² (93 m²). The blade racks in Figure 2.47 are the six exterior racks on either side of the four support hardware racks.

The entire high density cluster area was completely segregated from the remainder of the data center below the raised-access floor. This, along with the general layout of the key components of the cooling solution, further optimized the cooling solution in two ways. First, a very high static pressure was generated at the perforated tile locations, shown as a series of quartered tiles at the bottom of Figure 2.47. Air was directed below the raised-access floor in the direction indicated by the arrows on the four air-conditioning units shown at the top of the figure. By partitioning the entire subfloor area, a dead-head situation was created in the perforated tile area that maximized static pressure and airflow rates. Second, because the CRACs were located in such close proximity to the rack exhausts, direct return of warm air to the unit intakes was ensured to optimize unit efficiency. Finally, the hot-aisle/cold-aisle principle was taken to the extreme —a wall completely separating the warm and cold sides of the cluster, shown as the thick black line in Figure 2.47, guaranteed an absolute minimum of warm air recirculation, a problem that plagues many modern-day data centers. Transfer air ducts were included in the ceiling between the cold aisle and hot aisle to prevent excessive pressurization. The CRAHs

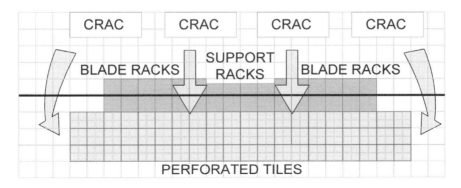

Figure 2.47 Revised cooling plan (includes rear-door heat exchangers; high density).

can supply more air than the blade servers will typically require (especially when four units are operating); therefore, bypass ducts were created to keep the CRAHs operating at maximum airflow.

Table 2.18 presents a comparison of key parameters between the original planned cooling solution and the hybrid solution that was ultimately implemented. It is clear that the introduction of a water-based rack option helped to create the desired showcase facility, with minimal floor space and air movement. The savings are quantified in the form of air-conditioning hardware savings and space savings (assuming that build-out of additional raised-access floor space would be required). A fringe benefit of this solution was additional savings in the form of operational costs. The overall efficiency of transferring heat with water is higher, and annual savings are indicated, assuming $0.08 per kWh.

MEASUREMENT AND RESULTS

A study was conducted in which temperatures were measured at multiple locations among the racks and CRAHs. The data showed this cooling method was highly effective at maintaining cool equipment inlet temperatures. An analysis of the temperatures showed that the RDHXs removed, on average, about 60% of the heat produced by the blade server racks. The remaining heat was removed by the CRAHs.

For the blade server racks, thermocouples were placed in three regions: equipment inlet (T_{EqpIn}), equipment outlet (T_{EqpOut}), and heat exchanger outlet (T_{HXOut}), as shown in Figure 2.48. Each region consisted of 18 thermocouples: three (left, middle, and right) for each of the six blade server chassis. The total number of temperature measurements for each blade rack was 54.

For the support racks, thermocouples were attached at two regions: equipment inlet and equipment outlet. Again, each region consisted of 18 thermocouples (left,

Table 2.18 Comparison of Key Parameters

Equipment	Original Cooling Plan	Revised Cooling Plan
Blades	1000	1000
Floor space, ft² (m²)	1600 (149)	1000 (93)
Total racks	16–28	16
Air-cooling tons, kBtu/h	85 (1020)	42.5 (510)
Water-cooling tons, kBtu/h	0	42.5 (510)
Total air cfm	42,000	21,000
Air-conditioning savings	N/A	$160,000
Space savings	N/A	$780,000
Operational savings per year	N/A	$21,000

middle, and right at six different heights). The total number of temperature measurements for each support rack was 36.

For the CRAHs, the inlet air temperatures were measured at 18 points across the intake and then averaged. The discharge temperatures were recorded from the CRAH control panel displays. The airflow rates were measured using a flowhood positioned atop the inlet.

The average temperature for each region of each blade server rack is shown in Table 2.19. Equipment inlet temperatures were very cool at 57.5°F to 60.4°F (14.2°C to 15.8°C). Note that each number in Table 2.19 is an average of 18 measurements. At the equipment inlets, the 18 measurements were typically very uniform (i.e., 97% of the measurements were within 0.5° of the average). The furthest outlier was 2.1°C above the average, which proves that this cooling method was effective at preventing hot-air recirculation over the tops and around the sides of the racks.

As the air exited the server blade chassis, it was significantly hotter at 86.9°F to 92.1°F (30.5°C to 33.4°C). As this heated air passed through the RDHXs, a portion of the heat was transferred to chilled water, allowing the air to exit the heat exchangers at more moderate temperatures in the range of 70.5°F to 72.9°F (21.4°C to 22.7°C).

Calculations for temperature change and energy are shown in Table 2.20. The temperature rise across the server blades ranged from 27.4°F to 32.9°F (15.2°C to 18.3°C), and the temperature drop across the RDHXs ranged from 16.2°F to 20.7°F

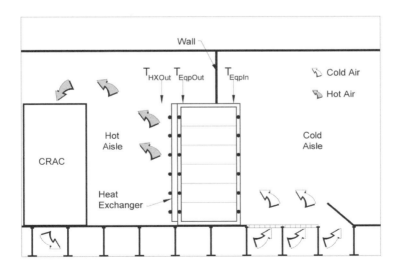

Figure 2.48 Schematic of cooling method and temperature measurements.

Table 2.19 Average Measured Temperatures for Blade Server Racks

Blade Rack #	T_{EqpIn}, °C	T_{EqpOut} (HX In), °C	T_{HXOut}, °C
1	14.2	31.0	21.4
2	14.5	31.6	21.7
3	15.1	32.1	21.6
4	14.9	32.8	22.2
5	15.2	33.4	21.9
6	15.0	32.6	22.4
7	15.2	32.3	22.1
8	15.4	32.3	21.6
9	15.7	32.6	22.1
10	15.8	33.4	22.7
11	15.5	33.0	22.1
12	15.2	30.5	21.5

Table 2.20 Calculations for Blade Server Racks

Blade Rack #	Temp. Rise Across Blades, °C	Temp. Drop Across RDHX, °C	Rack Airflow cfm	Blade Heat Load, kW	Extracted Heat, kW	Removed by RDHX, %
1	16.8	−9.6	1530	15.2	8.7	57%
2	17.0	−9.8	1530	15.4	8.9	58%
3	17.1	−10.5	1530	15.5	9.5	62%
4	17.8	−10.6	1530	16.2	9.6	59%
5	18.3	−11.5	1530	16.5	10.4	63%
6	17.6	−10.2	1530	15.9	9.2	58%
7	17.1	−10.2	1530	15.5	9.2	60%
8	17.0	−10.7	1530	15.3	9.7	63%
9	16.8	−10.4	1530	15.2	9.5	62%
10	17.7	−10.8	1530	16.0	9.8	61%
11	17.5	−10.9	1530	15.9	9.8	62%
12	15.2	−9.0	1530	13.8	8.1	59%

(9.0°C to 11.5°C). The airflow through each rack was estimated to be 1530 cfm (43.3 m^3/min), based on the blade server manufacturer's reported value of 255 cfm (7.2 m^3/min) per blade chassis. If temperature rise and airflow are known, then the heat, Q, produced by the blade servers can be calculated in watts as $Q = \text{cfm} \cdot \rho \cdot C_p \cdot \Delta T$, where $\rho = 1.25$ kg/m^3 and $C_p = 1003$ J/kg·K. Likewise, the heat removed by the RDHXs can be calculated using the same formula, with ΔT being the temperature drop across the rear door. The RDHXs removed 57% to 63% of the blade heat load.

Temperature data for the support racks are listed in Table 2.21. Equipment inlet temperatures were similar to those measured for the blade racks, which is expected. The temperature rise across the support equipment was low compared to the blades, which confirms the decision to leave the heat exchangers off of the support racks.

Information for the CRAHs is provided in Table 2.22. Here, ΔT is the difference between inlet and discharge. Heat removal is calculated using the same formula as before. The total heat removal using this analysis is 89.8 kW. For reference, the design airflow for the three nominal 20 ton units was 30,000 cfm (849.5 m^3/min).

The equipment inlet temperatures, as shown in Tables 2.19–2.21, were below the ASHRAE recommended range of 68°F–77°F (20°C–25°C). This suggests that the setpoint for the CRAH discharge temperature could be raised a few degrees. This would raise the equipment inlet temperatures and, in turn, raise the equipment outlet/heat exchanger inlet temperatures. The result would be a higher percentage of heat removed by the RDHXs because that mode of heat transfer is strongly influenced by the air/water temperature differential. Recall that it is more efficient to transfer heat with water versus air.

Table 2.21   Temperature Data for Support Racks

Support Rack Number	1	2	3	4
T_{Eqpln}	15.1	15.4	15.2	15.2
T_{EqpOut}	21.0	19.7	23.5	26.1
Temperature rise across equipment	5.9	4.3	8.3	10.9

Table 2.22   Measurements and Calculations for CRAHs

Measured Air Temp. and Flow Data	CRAH 41	CRAH 39	CRAH 38	CRAH 33	Total
CRAH inlet temps, °C	21.5	22.6	OFF	21.1	—
CRAH discharge temps, °C	15.2	15.2	OFF	15.2	—
CRAH ΔT, °C	6.3	7.4	OFF	5.9	—
CRAH flow rates, cfm	8120	7037	OFF	8378	23,535
CRAH heat removal, kW	30.0	30.7	OFF	29.1	89.8

A summary of the rack heat loads and the heat removal calculations is provided in Table 2.23. The actual heat loads at the time of the study were 67% of the planned loads. The heat removed by the CRAHs is calculated by subtracting the heat removed by the RDHXs from the actual heat loads. The resulting total for CRAH heat removal is in close agreement with the figure calculated in Table 2.22, which was based on mass flow rate and ΔT.

SUMMARY

Increasing heat densities and the desire to pack more computing power into smaller spaces created a number of challenges for deploying a powerful supercomputer at the Georgia Institute of Technology Center for the Study of Systems Biology. The facility was required to be of showcase quality, with fully utilized floor space, as well as minimal discomfort from noise and air movement. A hybrid cooling solution featuring a water-based rear-door heat exchanger proved to be the most effective way to create an optimal solution within the parameters given. The device is capable of removing 50% to 60% of the heat load within a rack, allowing for maximum packing density for the blades in the cluster and an optimal floor space requirement of 1000 ft^2 (93 m^2). The total requirement for air conditioning was cut roughly in half, minimizing cooling hardware and air-moving requirements. This solution will serve as an effective model for how end users can achieve high density cooling solutions as they transition from today's data center facilities to future designs.

Summary of best practices:

- Complete separation of hot and cold airstreams

- Water-cooling technology for net space reduction

- Floor tile design and layout to maximize airflow

- Eliminates flow obstructions in the raised-access floor plenum

- Segregation of high density area from remainder of data center

Table 2.23   Summary of Rack Heat Loads and Heat Removal Calculations

	Blades Racks, kW	Support Racks, kW	Total, kW
Planned heat load (from Table 1)	278.0	21.0	299.0
Actual heat load	186.4*	14.0**	200.4
Actual heat removed by RDHX	112.4*	0.0	112.4
Heat removed by CRACs	74.0	14.0	88.0

* From Table 2.20
** Reported by equipment

2.4.2   CASE STUDY 8—HEWLETT-PACKARD RICHARDSON DATACOOL™ DATA CENTER

This case study is based on the work of Hewlett Packard and Emerson Energy Systems in 1999 and 2000 (Stahl and Belady 2001; Patel et al. 2001) to develop a state-of-the-art cooling system. The final product, called DataCool, was deployed in HP's Richardson Data Center. As in most cases with product development, the base technology for the development was an existing cooling system known as Tele-Cool™ (Stahl 1993; Stahl and Zirath 1992). This overhead room cooling system (see Figure 2.49) is a distributed cooling system, first developed in the late 1970s, with more than 600 switch room installations worldwide since its introduction.

TeleCool's passive room cooling system (i.e., uses natural convection) is fluid based and capable of cooling 317 Btu/h·ft^2 (93 W/ft^2) in switch rooms. Although this passive technology did not work well in high heat load forced-convection environments, it provided the foundation for the development of the next generation cooling system that was ideal for high heat load rooms. Leveraging an already proven system architecture and infrastructure, it allowed two important advantages: shorter development time and fewer development resources. When HP and Emerson Energy Systems evaluated the maximum capacity of the natural convection system, many ideas for improving the capacity emerged. These improvements were to implement either ducts or fans on the coil, or a combination of the two.

The most promising ideas were modeled using CFD and validated using practical tests and measurements. As a result of this work, the concept shown in Figure 2.50 was selected. The conceptual idea is that hot air is drawn up through

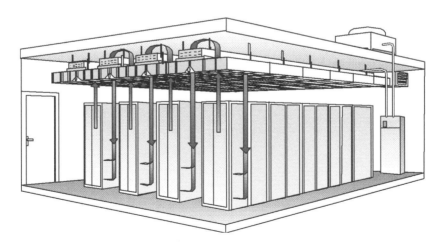

Figure 2.49 The natural convection based cooling system, TeleCool.

the horizontal heat exchanger and then sucked back down by the fans, providing a two-pass cooling solution. The idea was further analyzed in detail and optimized using CFD. For example, the ratio between the open coil area and the area covered by the fan trays, as well as the optimum distance between the top of the coil and the top of the enclosure, were optimized on prototypes using both theoretical calculations and practical measurements.

The fan-coil prototype, with dimensions of 5.9 ft (1.8 m) wide, 5.9 ft (1.8 m) deep, and 1.6 ft (0.5 m) high, consisted of an enclosure, an air-to-fluid coil, fan trays with axial fans, and an electrical module. The air passed through the coil twice, first upward and then down and through the fans. Since the two fan trays can be moved horizontally, the cold air can be directed toward the air inlet of the equipment, depending on the location of the cold aisle (see Figure 2.51). For testing, DC fans

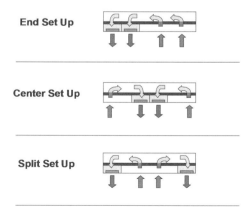

Figure 2.50 Fan-coil.

Figure 2.51 Side view of basic fan tray configurations.

with a total maximum capacity of approximately 7000 ft³/min (12000 m³/h) were chosen because they were easy to control; AC fans were available as an alternative.

LAYOUT OF DATA CENTER

Prototype Room Test Bed

In order to prove the technology, HP and Emerson Energy Systems completed extensive CFD modeling before committing the resources to build a prototype test room (Stahl 1993). The test room was built as a subroom in a raised-access floor data center and was approximately 452 ft² (42 m²), with three rows of six racks (for a total of 18 racks) as shown by Figures 2.52–2.54. The room was 12.8 ft (3.9 m) high. Each rack (6.4 ft [1.95 m] high, 3 ft [0.91 m] deep, and 2 ft [0.61 m] wide) had four resistive loads at 12,000 Btu/h (3.6 kW), each, for a total of up to 49,000 Btu/h (14.4 kW) per rack. Each rack also had a total of 12 axial fans mounted on the intake side of the rack that generated a total airflow of about 2000 Btu/h (3400 m³/h). These loads and fans simulated the airflow for typical high-performance servers of the future, such as blades. The total heat load that could be generated in this room was 887,000 Btu/h (260 kW). Using the total floor size of the room in the calculation, this is equal to 1960 Btu/h·ft² (574 W/ft²).

Figure 2.52 Photo of the prototype room.

Figure 2.53 Photo from the prototype room.

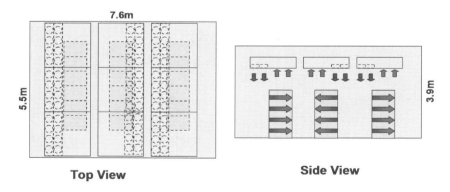

Top View　　　　　**Side View**

Figure 2.54 Prototype room layout.

In the room, nine prototype fan-coils were installed and hydraulically connected (see Figure 2.55). The figure shows one of the three fluid circuits and the interleaved layout of the fan-coils to aid in redundancy. Each coolant distribution unit (CDU) was connected to three fan-coils. If there was a failure of one CDU, the remaining two provided the cooling. The room had typical office walls mounted on the intake side of the rack with approximately 68°F (20°C) surrounding temperature. The floor

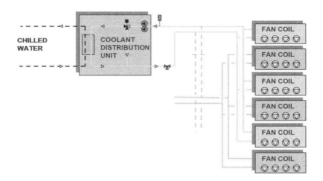

Figure 2.55 Typical hydraulic system diagram with interleaved fan-coils.

in the test room was a solid raised-access floor with air under the floor approximately 55°F (13°C). However, during the hybrid testing, perforated floor tiles were installed to study the impact of running DataCool™ together with traditional raised-access floor cooling.

System Construction

The CDU houses the heat exchanger between the system fluid to the building chilled fluid, the control valve, the dual redundant pumps, and the system controls. The CDU was typically housed in the facility mechanical room and controls all aspects of the system, so that the room temperature was kept constant. However, since the fluid temperature was never allowed to go below the dew point, only sensible cooling was required by the fan-coils. Each of the fluid circuits also had a fluid management system to detect any fluid flow disturbance and immediately evacuate the fluid in the circulation loop, if necessary.

MEASUREMENT TOOLS

In order to evaluate the cooling capacity of the room temperature, probes were located at four different heights (1.57 ft [0.48 m], 3.1 ft [0.94 m], 4.6 ft [1.4 m] and 6.1 ft [1.85 m] above the floor) at the air intake for each rack monitored. In addition, room temperatures, fluid temperatures, and air humidity were monitored during the test/verification.

MEASUREMENT METHODOLOGY AND RESULTS

Capacity Testing

For a certain airflow through each fan-coil, the electric heat loads in the racks were sequentially turned on until temperatures reached a specified maximum air temperature at any of the 72 temperature probes. At that point, the heat capacity was determined by measuring the amp draw to the electric heaters in the racks. The heat load capacity of the room was based on when one of the inlet temperatures exceeded a specified 86°F (30°C) ambient temperature.

The capacity testing was performed with several basic equipment configurations (see Figure 2.56):

1. Horizontal rack airflow with hot-aisle/cold-aisle setup
2. Horizontal rack airflow with inlet to outlet/inlet to outlet setup
3. Horizontal rack intake and vertical top exhaust

Brief Test Results. Table 2.24 shows the maximum heat load cooled by the system when the maximum inlet temperature to any of the 18 racks, at any height, reached 86°F (30°C).

Failure Modes

To understand the resiliency of the technology, several failure modes were simulated during the test.

a. Three (of nine) fan-coils turned off in a row
b. Three (of nine) fan-coils turned off in a perpendicular row
c. Three (of nine) fan-coils turned off in a diagonal row
d. One (of nine) fan-coils turned off in the center
e. One (of nine) fan-coils turned off in the corner

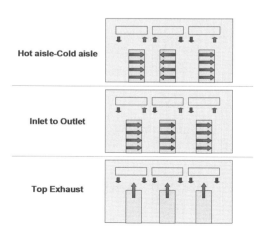

Figure 2.56 Side view of basic equipment configurations.

Figure 2.57 shows which units were turned off as a function of location during each test.

Brief Test Results. Table 2.25 shows the temperature difference between the maximum inlet temperature to any of the 18 racks, at any height, at normal conditions, and the maximum inlet temperature to any of the 18 racks, at any height, after one hour of failure mode. The heat load was 3080 W/m^2, and approximate airflow for each fan-coil in operation was 6474 ft^3/min (11,000 m^3/h).

Note that the loss of one unit has minimal impact on the temperatures in the room, while a loss of 33% of the cooling had a much larger impact.

Transients for Catastrophic Failure

Transient testing was done for different heat loads to collect empirical data for comparison with theoretical calculations. Since the transient values are logged with the cooling system off, the data are more dependent on the test room and the equip-

Table 2.24 Heat Load at Different Equipment Configurations

Configuration	Airflow Per Coil, ft^3/min (m^3/h)	Heat Load, W/ft^2 (W/m^2)
Hot aisle-cold aisle	6474 (11,000)	470 (5060)
Inlet to outlet	6474 (11,000)	286 (3080)
Top exhaust	4708 (8000)	295 (3170)

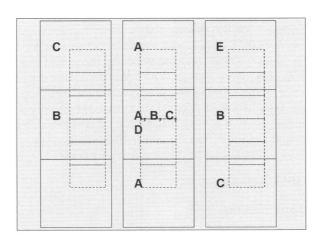

Figure 2.57 Top view indication of fan-coils turned off during failure mode testing.

Table 2.25   Temperature Difference at Different Failure Modes

Failure Mode	Temperature Difference, °C
A	16
B	7
C	17
D	1
E	1

ment in the room than the cooling system itself. A summary of the results can be seen in Figure 2.58.

Gradients

Gradients were logged during some of the tests in order to verify the thermal behavior of the cooling system in the room.

Brief Test Results. Figure 2.59, shows the maximum difference in temperature for four vertical points in the room for a hot-aisle/cold-aisle equipment configuration and 3080 W/m^2 heat load. The approximate airflow for each fan-coil was 4708 ft^3/min (8000 m^3/h). Temperatures in bold are for points 1.57 ft (0.48 m), 3.1 ft (0.94 m), 4.6 ft (1.4 m) and 6.1 ft (1.85 m) above the floor. Temperatures in Roman type are for points 0.16 ft (0.05 m), 3.0 ft (0.9 m), 6.0 ft (1.83 m), and 8.0 ft (2.44 m) above the floor.

Hybrid System

The capacity of the existing DataCool system together with the raised-access floor was tested in two steps. First, the capacity of the existing raised-access floor was tested with as many perforated floor tiles as could practically be installed. Next, the combined capacity of the existing raised-access floor and DataCool system was tested.

Brief Test Results. Table 2.26 shows the heat load when the maximum inlet temperature to any of the 18 racks at any height reached 86°F (30°C) for raised-access floor and for a hybrid of raised-access floor and DataCool together. The approximate airflow for each fan-coil was 4708 ft^3/min (8000 m^3/h).

Note the hybrid test shows that the two cooling schemes can coexist to boost capacity even further, in this case by 317 Btu/h·ft^2 (1 kW/m^2).

ANALYSIS AND COMPARISONS

CFD Model Construction

A CFD tool called Flovent (Flometrics 1999) was used to model the prototype data center. The numerical computational domain was the overall room. As shown in Figure 2.60, the racks were modeled as enclosures with an inset rectangular block called a *cuboid* (Flometrics 1999). The cuboid had four sets of recirculating openings,

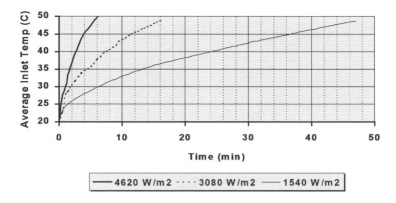

Figure 2.58 Transients at different heat loads with no cooling.

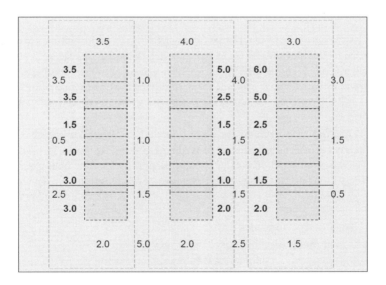

Figure 2.59 Top view of gradients in °C.

Table 2.26   Heal Load for Different Systems

System Configuration	Heat Load, W/ft^2 (W/m^2)
Raised floor	176 (1890)
Raised floor + Datacool^{TM}	565 (6080)

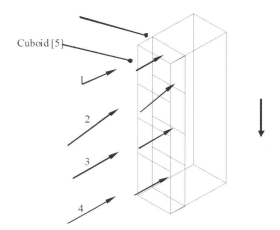

Cuboid [5]

2

3

4

Figure 2.60 Simplified definition of a rack in the model.

as shown by the arrows labeled 1–4 in Figure 2.60. Each recirculating opening pair was assigned a flow of 600 cfm (0.28 m³/s). Alternating pairs were assigned a heat load of either 0 or 12,284 Btu/h (3600 W) such that only two compartments within a rack were at full power, and each rack was dissipating 24,567 Btu/h (7200 W). The rack, thus defined, was arrayed across the room with geometry as defined in the proto-type data center.

The DataCool heat exchangers were modeled as shown in Figure 2.61. The appropriate heat transfer attributes were assigned to simulate the performance of the real heat exchangers based on earlier characterization tests. The heat transfer attributes are identified in terms of the effectiveness, ε, of the cooling coil. The following are the key attributes:

- Heat exchanger effectiveness, ε
- Mass flow through each heat exchanger unit
- Temperature of the coolant to each heat exchanger unit, $T_{c,in}$

The heat transferred to the coolant is given by the following equation:

$$Q_{hex} = \varepsilon(mc_p)_{min}(T_{h,in} - T_{c,in})$$

where ε is the effectiveness of the heat exchanger, (mc_p) is the capacity of the fluid, the subscript *min* refers to the fluid (hot air from room or cooling fluid) with the minimum capacity, and $T_{c,in}$ is the inlet temperature of the cooling fluid. In our example, the hot air from the room, drawn through each heat exchanger, is the one with minimum capacity.

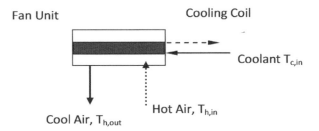

Figure 2.61 Heat exchanger definition.

The heat exchanger characteristics were defined based on the following:

- Airflow rate, $T_{h,in}$, and coolant temperature, $T_{c,in}$
- Effectiveness, ε, and capacity of air, C_{min}

Figure 2.62 is an image of the DataCool CFD model, and Figure 2.63 compares the DataCool model to the actual deployment in the prototype data center. The heat exchanger's three-dimensional geometry is created using the Enclosure, Cuboid, and Volume Resistance object types in Flovent (Flometrics 1999). A recirculating opening is applied with following heat exchanger characteristics:

- Heat exchanger effectiveness = 0.6 (calculated using approach shown in Bash [2000])
- Airflow rate = 4500 ft³/min (2.12 m³/s) (through each DataCool unit)
- Inlet coolant temperature = 62.6°F (17°C) (inlet to DataCool heat exchanger) (varies; the appropriate value is used for each unit)

The racks and heat exchangers, thus defined, are arrayed across the room to form the room model as shown in Figure 2.64. The room is modeled as adiabatic with no-slip boundary conditions (Flometrics 1999). A grid is applied across the model as a last step in preprocessing.

CFD Modeling Assumptions and Key Measures

The CFD modeling was conducted with the intent of gaining an understanding of flow patterns and establishing an average value of inlet air temperature into the compartments modeled in the rack. The DataCool heat exchangers were allowed to operate based on the attributes defined in the earlier section. The modeling calculated $T_{h,in}$ and $T_{h,out}$, the terminal air temperatures into and out of the heat exchangers. With the average air-terminal temperature into the heat exchanger, one can determine the heat extracted by each heat exchanger unit. The sum of heat extracted

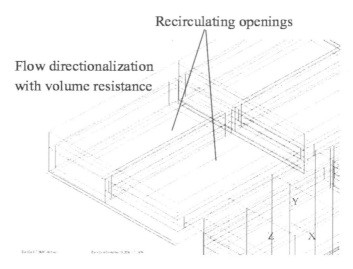

Figure 2.62 Representation of the heat exchanger in the model.

Figure 2.63 Image of the heat exchanger modules in the prototype data center.

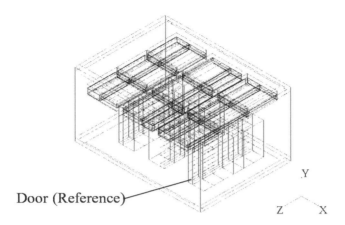

Figure 2.64 Model of the prototype data center.

by all the heat exchangers should be equal to the heat dissipated in the room. Such an energy balance was used as a preliminary check of the modeling.

Results

The simulation results are compared with measurements obtained from the prototype data center. Figure 2.65 is a plan view of the room. Locations in which comparisons were made are given numerical designations (circled). In addition, racks are labeled for a subsequent comparison. Heights of 0.16 ft (0.05 m), 3.3 ft (1.0 m), and 6.6 ft (2.0 m) from the floor are compared between measured and modeled data.

Figures 2.66–2.68 display the results of the plan view comparisons at the indicated heights. At $Y = 0.16$ ft (0.05 m), both the experimental and numerical results show hot spots in the room in areas 1–5 and 10. Thermal gradients within the room are also in general agreement, with absolute values showing less agreement. Locations 7 and 11, in particular, exhibit disagreement in absolute value as well as trends. Similar results are observed at $Y = 3.3$ ft (1.0 m) with discrepancies in absolute values instead occurring at points 2 and 6. Similar agreement is shown at $Y = 6.6$ ft (2.0 m). The primary areas of disagreement between the numerical and experimental results are most likely a result of simplifications made to the model in combination with the removal of incidental physical detail, such as tubing and ceiling members. A major result of the analysis, which is also in agreement with the experiment, is that the portion of the room opposite the door (locations 1–6 and 10 in Figure 2.65) is hotter than that near the door, especially near the floor. This

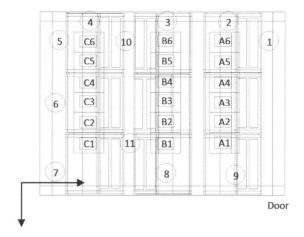

Figure 2.65 Plan view of rooms showing comparison locations.

is due to the asymmetric spacing of the rack rows in the Z direction and may not be obvious without the aid of analysis by the individual responsible for designing the room layout and cooling infrastructure.

Figure 2.69 compares selected experimental and numerical inlet temperatures. Rather than report inlet data for all 72 compartments, potential problem areas were identified (Figures 2.66–2.68) by looking for hot spots in the plan views. Correspondingly, inlet temperatures were examined in regions where hot spots were found. In Figure 2.69, components within a rack are numbered from bottom to top (position 1 is the bottom-most component, position 4 the top-most). Results indicate that the simulation adequately captures the experimental pattern. Both inlet temperatures and rack-level thermal gradients correlate well with the experiment and accurately indicate where improvements in the thermal management of the room can be made.

SUMMARY

This case study outlines the work done in Hewlett-Packard's Richardson data center for high density cooling. The work demonstrates some important points:

1. Over 557 W/ft^2 (6000W/m^2) was achievable with racks at 49,000 Btu/h (14.4 kW) using overhead cooling with some underfloor makeup air. At the time, this was unprecedented density and proved that high density cooling is viable.

2. The apparent capacity of the data center can be improved even with overhead cooling by transitioning from all servers facing the same way to a hot-aisle/ cold-aisle configuration. The apparent cooling capacity went from 286 W/ft^2

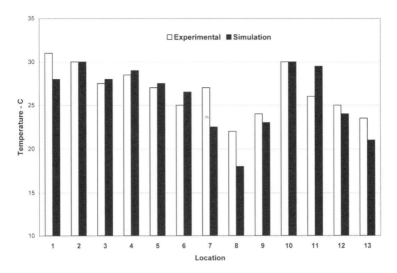

Figure 2.66 Temperature map at Y = 0.16 ft (0.05 m).

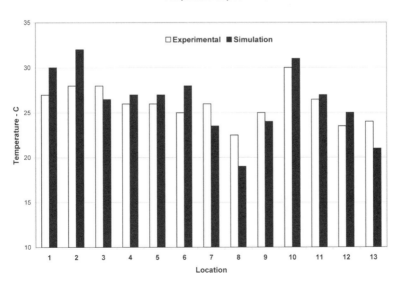

Figure 2.67 Temperature map at Y = 3.3 ft (1.0 m).

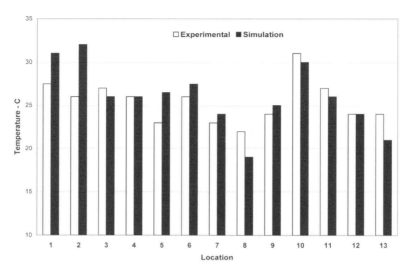

Figure 2.68 Temperature map at Y = 6.6 ft (2.0 m).

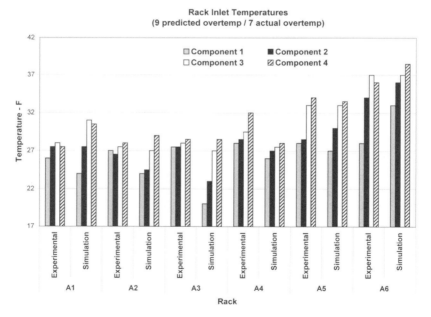

Figure 2.69 Selected rack inlet temperatures.

(3080 W/m^2) to 470 W/ft^2 (5060 W/m^2). This was a 64% improvement by using industry hot-aisle/cold-aisle best practices.

3. Failure of cooling in high density applications will show rapid increase in temperature, which needs to be provided for in the back-up strategy.

4. This work also validated the use of computational fluid dynamics in data center environments.

REFERENCES

Bash, C.B. 2000. A hybrid approach to plate fin-tube heat exchanger analysis. *Proceedings of the International Conference and Exhibition on High Density Interconnect and Systems Packaging, Denver, Colorado,* pp. 40–8.

Flometrics. 1999. Flovent version 2.1. Flometrics Ltd., Surrey, England.

Patel, C., C. Bash, C. Belady, L. Stahl, and D. Sullivan. 2001. Computational fluid dynamics modeling of high density data centers to assure systems inlet air specifications. *Proceedings of InterPACK 2001 Conference, Kauai, Hawaii.*

Stahl, L. 1993. Switch room cooling—A system concept with switch room located cooling equipment. *Proceedings of INTELEC 1993, Paris, France.*

Stahl, L., and C. Belady. 2001. Designing an alternative to conventional room cooling. *Proceedings of the 2001 International Telecommunications Energy Conference, Edinburgh, Scotland.*

Stahl, L., and H. Zirath. 1992. TELECOOL, A new generation of cooling systems for switching equipment. *Ericsson Review* 4:124–92.

2.5 RAISED-ACCESS FLOOR WITH UNDERFLOOR SUPPLY/DUCTED CEILING RETURN

2.5.1 CASE STUDY 9—ORACLE DATA CENTER

This case study highlights the importance of creating a physical barrier between cold supply (see Figure 2.70) and hot return air on the data center floor. A conventional hot-aisle/cold-aisle rack configuration in data centers has worked well when rack power loads are low—typically less than 4 kW per rack. However, with increasing rack loads, excess cold air must be supplied to the cold aisle to reduce hot spots near the top of the racks that result from hot air diffusing into the cold aisle. A large fraction of the excess cold air also bypasses the electronic equipment and returns back to the air conditioning units. This practice is energy inefficient; it increases fan energy use and requires more energy to produce colder air. A physical barrier between hot and cold air streams within a data center is needed to avoid mixing of cold air with hot air. A new approach to physically separate the cold and hot air streams within a rack was selected and implemented in a high power density section of a large data center. The selection was based on energy as well as other practical considerations.

Figure 2.70 Rack layout showing the cold supply-air row

This case study discusses the high-density rack hot-air containment approach—the rationale for its design and its advantages and limitations—and presents data on its energy performance.

The field performance of the high power density section of a large enterprise-level data center is reported here. This data center was constructed in phases. The first phase used the then state-of-the-art practice of hot-aisle/cold-aisle rack arrangement on the data center floor. The chilled-water CRACs are located on both ends of the rack aisles and supplied cold air under the raised floor. Supply air is delivered to cold aisles through perforated tiles in front of the equipment racks. Hot air from the equipment racks is discharged into the hot aisle, from which it is drawn back into the CRAC units. Our field observations confirmed the increased supply air temperatures to equipment near the top of the racks since the discharged air from hot aisles was being drawn back in to the cold aisles. We also noticed that some of the cold air did not go through the electronic equipment but was instead drawn directly back to the CRACs without providing any cooling. A further review of data for total airflow from the CRACs and total airflow required for the electronic-equipment cooling indicated the CRACs supplied far more air than was required.

The data center design and operations team decided to address the above issues during the design and construction of the second-phase expansion of the data center in 2003. The expansion included a 12,000 ft^2 (1115 m^2) high power density area with an average rack power of 6.8 kW per rack for 640 racks, or an average power load of 170 W/ft^2 (16 W/m^2). The team decided to increase the cooling energy efficiency by reducing unnecessary airflow on the data center floor; by supplying enough cold air to match the airflow requirements of the electronic equipment, the airflow rates would be reduced to less than one-half those of the existing system. In order for us to adjust airflow demand to electronic equipment, which would vary as new equipment was brought in or older equipment was removed, we decided to install variable-speed drives on the CRAC fans. However, CFD modeling showed that slowing the airflow increased the risk of hot-air infiltration in the cold aisle, causing high supply air temperatures, especially near the top of the rack and racks on the end of the aisle. The high temperatures, in turn, required even colder supply air temperatures, thus negating some of the energy efficiency gains from the airflow reduction. The team decided to create a physical barrier between the hot and cold air on the data floor to prevent mixing. This also allowed us to raise our supply temperature without concern for reaching unacceptably high temperatures near the top of the rack due to hot-air infiltration if there was no physical separation. The team considered different arrangements of barriers between hot and cold air, such as cold-aisle containment and hot-aisle containment, but elected to use a rack enclosure with a discharge duct to ceiling return air plenum.

The system worked very well and provided excellent energy savings with measured simple payback of less than six months. The fact that the CRAC fan speeds could be adjusted to meet the equipment load requirement, and the equipment in the data center was loaded gradually over a period of time, meant that the fans could run more slowly. This reduced the direct energy use and indirect cooling energy use required to remove heat generated by fans.

The system utilizes raised-floor access air supply and hot-air containment through a rack exhaust duct to a ceiling return plenum. A supplemental fan in the exhaust duct aids in overcoming additional pressure loss. The floor layout is divided into five 2400 ft^2 (233 m^2) sections. For this study, the environmental attributes— rack power loads, floor-tile flow rates, IT equipment flow rates, IT equipment intake, and exhaust air temperatures—for one of the five 2400 ft^2 (233 m^2) sections were collected and analyzed. Spot measurements were also taken from the four other 2,400 ft^2 (233 m^2) sections, which reinforced the reported data for the first section.

LAYOUT OF DATA CENTER

There are seven rows, each with approximately 20 racks between the opposing CRACs in each of the five high-power density sections. Each section utilizes five 40 ton (140.68 kW) chilled-water CRACs, as shown as Figure 2.71.

The racks are positioned in the conventional hot-aisle/cold-aisle arrangement, although all racks could face the same direction since there are no hot aisles due to

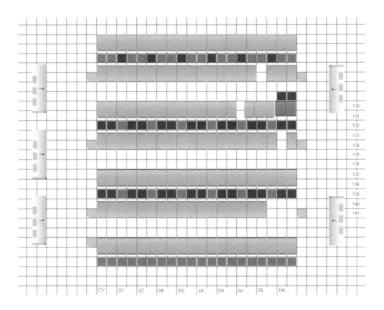

Figure 2.71 One of five high-power density areas showing rack layout, CRAC locations, and floor tile locations. Tiles shown in the darker shade represent floor grate locations.

the heat containment exhaust duct. The rack widths are 2 ft (0.61 m), rack heights are 7.33 ft (2.24 m), and rack depths are 42 in. (1.07 m). The 2 ft (0.61 m) floor pitch is maintained with a 3 ft (0.91 m) aisle for air delivery and a 4 ft (1.22 m) aisle between the rears of the racks. With some variation, each rack has a typical config- uration of servers and a single small network switch. The racks have solid rear doors with solid bottom and side panels and cable seals to eliminate cool air bypass into the warm exhaust/return airstream. A 20 in. (0.51 m) round duct on top of each rack connects to the return air plenum. It contains a 16 in. (0.406 m) low-power variable- speed fan (maximum 90 W) with a maximum airflow rate of approximately 1600 cfm (45.3 m^3/min).

The raised-access floor height is 30 in. (0.76 m), and there are no significant underfloor blockages to consider for this study. Measured flow rates from the open floor tiles and grates confirm good underfloor pressure distribution.

The return air plenum is located 12 ft (3.66 m) above the raised-access floor and is constructed using standard drop-ceiling materials with a 24 in. (0.61 m) grid pattern to match the floor tiles. The roof structure is 25 ft (7.62 m) above the raised- access floor. There is an additional fire-rated drop ceiling 5 ft (1.52 m) below the roof structure, leaving a return air plenum height of 8 ft (2.44 m), as shown in Figure 2.72. During a utility failure, balancing vents installed in the ceiling plenum vertical wall allow air to exit the plenum into the open area of the data center before returning to

Figure 2.72 Rack layout with exhaust duct from racks to ceiling plenum.

the CRACs. This longer return path extends the cooling through an increased thermal mass and, thus, extends critical operation during a utility failure.

The 40 ton (140 kW) variable-speed chilled-water CRACs are connected to the return air plenum using extensions, as shown in Figure 2.72. The CRAC temperature/humidity sensor was removed from the typical return air location in the CRAC and moved to the underfloor supply air plenum approximately 10 ft (3.05 m) in front of the CRAC. The CRAC control was changed from return air temperature setpoint control to supply air temperature setpoint control. The setpoint for the CRAC supply temperature is currently 68°F (20°C). CRAC unit RH sensing mode is changed from relative (direct) to absolute (predictive) to allow more stable control of RH. CRAC variable frequency drive (VFD) in each section maintains underfloor pressure at a setpoint of 0.04 in. (1.016 mm) w.c. CRACs are controlled by a BMS utilizing differential pressure sensors located under the floor and operated on proportional-integral-derivative control loop for steady operation. A separate central air-handling system provides makeup air, facility pressurization, and humidity control.

MEASUREMENT INSTRUMENTS

Power measurements were taken using a Fluke 434 three-phase power quality analyzer. Airflow measurements were collected using a Lutron AM-4204A hot-wire anemometer and a 0–0.25 in. (0–6.35 mm) WC Magnahelic® differential pressure gauge. Temperature measurements were collected using an Extech model 421501 hand-held thermometer utilizing a type K thermocouple.

MEASUREMENT METHODOLOGY

Power

Rack power was measured at the 208 V three-phase branch circuit breakers. Rack power is dual fed, so a simple addition of the A and B feed power results in the total rack power. Incidentally, power measurements collected were, on average, 60% of the power reported by the hardware nameplate data.

Temperature

Temperature measurements were collected at three vertical locations 2 in. away from the IT equipment intake grills. IT equipment exhaust temperatures were spot checked and compared to the averaged rack exhaust temperature. In most cases, the average rack exhaust temperature was a few degrees lower than the hottest IT equipment exhaust temperature. Understanding that the IT equipment exhaust grills vary in location and size for the different functions of the equipment, resulting in a variety of temperatures and airflow rates, the slight drop in rack exhaust temperature as an aggregate made sense and was accepted. Analyzing supply air temperatures to rack inlet temperatures will give a good indication of hot-air recirculation. Analyzing return temperatures from the IT hardware to the CRACs will give good insight into bypass air conditions.

Airflow

Floor tile supply air measurements were collected using a hot-wire anemometer across a traverse plane and were compared to a measured underfloor pressure at the tile and the corresponding flow rate as supplied by the tile manufacturer. The hot-wire readings were collected and averaged using the equal-area method of traversing a 2 by 2 and 4 ft (0.61 by 0.61 and 1.62 m) tall exhaust duct placed over the floor tile. Rack airflow rates were calculated using the heat-transfer equation from measured total rack load and temperature rise. The racks airflow rates are balanced to a slightly negative pressure to ensure the rack flow rate had a similar flow rate as the IT equipment load. This ensured little-to-no bypass air would dilute the rack temperature rise reading. An attempt was made to validate the IT equipment airflow rates using the hot-wire anemometer across a traverse plane created with a 17 by 7 and 24 in. (43.18 by 17.78 and 60.96 cm) intake duct placed over and sealed around two server face plates. The velocity measurements were too unstable to measure accurately and, in the physical space, it was not possible to extend the traverse plane duct. With the rack exhaust fan airflow rate equivalent to the aggregate server airflow rates for the rack due to a zero or slightly negative differential pressure in the rear rack plenum, there was confidence in the single method of data collection.

MEASURED DATA

Figures 2.73–2.82 provide a comparison of power, temperature, and airflow for the four selected rows within the high density section. For each of the four rows, the data graphs will first provide a comparison of rack power and rack intake/exhaust temperatures. The CRAC return temperatures are included in this section for the purpose of understanding any dilution of the air temperature as it left the equipment rack. The next comparison features tile airflow rates and rack airflow rates, including a total aggregate of the tile supply and rack flow. Finally, the CRAC fan speed and power usage are measured and recorded and compared to CRAC full-on power consumption (see Table 2.27).

ANALYSIS

Airflow Distribution

Well distributed airflow through floor tiles is attributed to CRAC fan control using VFD to maintain a consistent underfloor pressure and supply air. Balancing the volume of air delivery to optimize cooling provisioning was necessary by adjusting the quantity of 56% open floor grates. Fourteen grate and six perforated tiles allowed the CRACs to operate at 51 Hz or 86% fan speed to deliver 63,684 cfm (1803 $m^3/$ min), providing a 6% oversupply. More work is required to balance all rows and

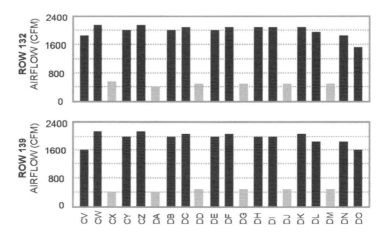

Figure 2.73 Underfloor supply air volume flow. Gray bars: 25% open floor tiles; black bars: 58% open floor tiles.

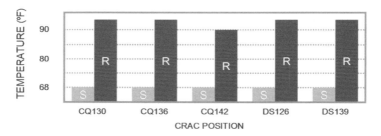

Figure 2.74 CRAC supply and return-air temperatures. Gray bars: supply air temperature; black bars: return air temperature.

sections within the high density area to achieve near unity balance. The cold row originally had six perforated tiles and fourteen grate tiles, which provided 44,000 cfm (1246 m³/min) for the two aisles analyzed. The supply rate was not sufficient for the IT equipment load, which required 59,877 cfm (1696 m³/min), leaving a shortage of 16,000 cfm (453 m³/min). In a conventional cooling arrangement, this 26% under-provisioning of cooling would have caused the inlet temperatures to exceed recommended standards; however, the inlet temperatures continued to stay below 77°F (25°C) due to the heat containment system. Using all 56% grates provided 82,000 cfm (1096 m³/min) for the two aisles analyzed. The supply rate exceeded the IT equipment load requirement, delivering an oversupply of 12,000 cfm (340 m³/min) or 36%

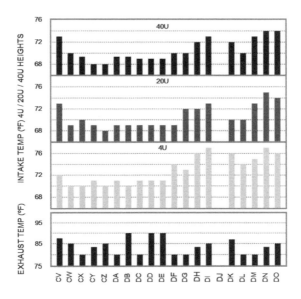

Figure 2.75 Row 130 rack intake and exhaust temperatures.

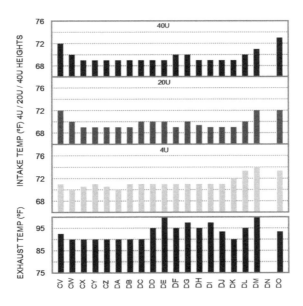

Figure 2.76 Row 134 rack intake and exhaust temperatures.

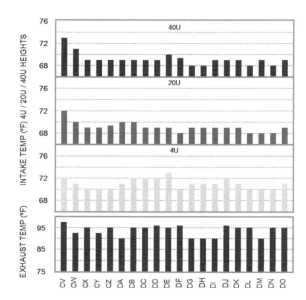

Figure 2.77 Row 137 rack intake and exhaust temperatures.

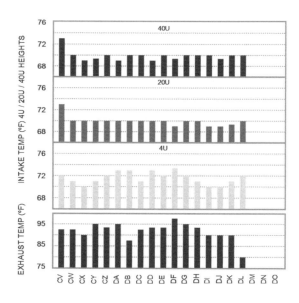

Figure 2.78 Row 141 rack intake and exhaust temperatures.

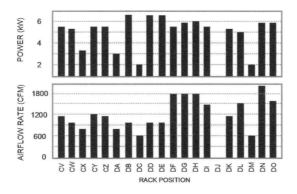

Figure 2.79 Row 130 rack power and airflow rate.

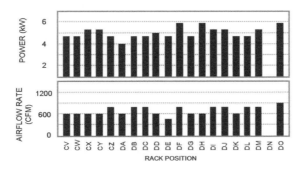

Figure 2.80 Row 134 rack power and airflow rate.

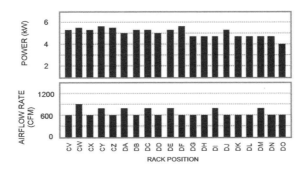

Figure 2.81 Row 137 rack power and airflow rate.

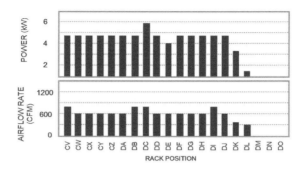

Figure 2.82 Row 141 rack power and airflow rate.

Table 2.27   CRAC Fan Speed and Power[1]

CRAC Control	Power, kW	Fan Speed, %	Frequency, Hz	Underfloor Pressure, In. W.C.
NONE	11.20	100	60	0.055
VFD	7.10	86	51	0.040
VFD	4.73	75	45	0.035

1. CRAC fans operate at the 51 Hz or 86% fan speed to maintain 0.04 in. (1.016 mm) w.c. for sufficient air supply provisioning. Power use at this operating point is 7.1 kW.

overprovisioning. CRACs for this arrangement were operating at full speed to maintain the setpoint for underfloor pressure. (See Figure 2.83.)

Air Temperature Distribution

The air temperature at the intake grills of the IT equipment was very consistent due to supply air temperature control and all return air/heat being contained and directed back to the CRAC. Intake temperatures ranged between the supply temperatures of 68°F (20°C) and the ASHRAE (2004) class 1 upper limit of 77°F (25°C), with the warmer temperatures residing at the *lower* rack height positions and toward the ends of the row. The consistently warmer temperatures at lower rack intake positions were attributed to entrainment of warm air from under racks into cool supply air due to Venturi effects caused by high velocity airstreams through floor grates (see Figure 2.84).

The warm airstream passing between the rack frame and floor was validated by measurement. Rack DK134, which had a raised intake temperatures of 71.6°F

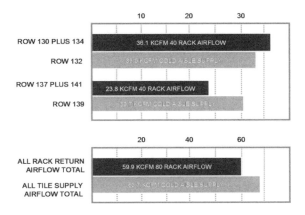

Figure 2.83 Row airflow supply and rack airflow return aggregate.

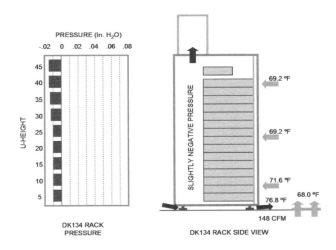

Figure 2.84 Venturi effect on temperatures from high velocity supply through floor grates.

(22°C), demonstrated this effect with 148 cfm (4.2 m^3/min) of 76.8°F (24.9°C) air flowing from the rear to the front. CFD studies are required to further evaluate the effects of warm air entrainment at lower rack conditions due to Venturi effects caused by high-velocity floor grates.

Rack exhaust temperatures were measured and compared to the return air temperatures in order to validate little-to-no entrainment of cool air into the warm exhaust air. Rack exhaust and CRAC return temperature comparison is also important to understand effects of the 6% overprovisioning on reduction in return air temperature. An average of 4°F (2.22°C) reduction of CRAC return temperature versus rack exhaust temperature indicates near unity efficiency of air distribution. Additional work is required to balance the remaining sections of the high density area.

The IT equipment in rack positions DN and DO130 faces both the front and rear of the rack. In this configuration, the equipment on the back side of the rack pulls the intake air from what would typically be a hot aisle if hot air was not contained. In the containment approach, intake temperatures are within ASHRAE (2004) class 1 limits and are measured 76°F (24.4°C) at 4U, 71°F (21.67°C) at 20U, and 74°F (23.33°C) at 40U rack heights.

Rack Plenum Pressure

Rack exhaust fans running at full speed without any flow control produce a negative pressure (up to –0.055 in. [–1.397mm] w.c.) inside the rack for the loads sized in this case study. This is not the best operating scenario due to cold supply air being wasted and pulled into the rack, creating an artificially high rack air consumption rate and diluting the hot exhaust air to the CRACs, which lowers their performance. Efficient control of the rack airflow rate can be handled using two different methods—by choking down a basic manual damper installed in the ceiling tile connection until the pressure in the rack is raised to –0.01 in. (0.254 mm) w.c., or by using a fan speed controller, which controls fans to maintain a neutral rack plenum.

Racks containing exhaust air plenum without exhaust fans allow a positive pressure (up to +0.07 in. [1.78 mm] w.c.) within the rack plenum (see Figure 2.85). This was tested by removing fans in one of the racks. High positive pressure combined with the Venturi effect from high-velocity supply from floor grate produced 76°F (24.44°C) intake air at 4U height due to 174 cfm (4.9 m³/min) of 83.6°F (28.67°C) air mixing with 68°F (20°C) supply air at the front base of the rack.

The decision to set the rack plenum pressure at –0.01 to 0 in. (–0.254 to 0 mm) w.c. was chosen after multiple investigations. It was thought that running the plenum at a negative pressure would assist IT equipment fan performance and reduce IT equipment fan power. Such was not the case. For one IT equipment manufacturer, the fan power curve shows that the IT equipment fan power is fairly flat at all backpressures and flow rates. The amount of IT equipment fan power savings is negligible compared to the energy lost by pulling in bypass air through the rack cracks and openings, due to the negative pressure in the rack.

Stated power savings for CRAC fan power were 4.1 kW at 51 Hz operation (versus 60 Hz operation). For the total high density area, annual savings are $59,100 at $0.055 per kWh (see Table 2.28).

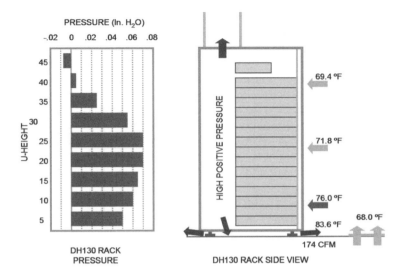

Figure 2.85 DH130 positive rack pressure effects on intake air.

Table 2.28   CRAC Fan Power and Additional Savings

CRAC Quantity	Power Savings, kW	Actual Cost Savings, @$0.055/kW·h
1	4.1	$1970
30	123.0	$59,100

Additional energy savings are possible based on higher supply air temperatures. Higher supply air temperatures allow higher chilled-water temperatures, which result in greater chiller efficiency and additional free hours of cooling.

SUMMARY

CFD modeling and published studies have shown that twice as much air at colder-than-required temperatures is being delivered to maintain the upper temperature limit of the ASHRAE (2004) class 1 standard. There is a significant cost associated with oversupply, as well as missed opportunity to efficiently operate the CRACs and chiller plant to further reduce operational costs. Over-provision of the cool supply air at temperatures below 68°F (20°C) did not allow ASHRAE class 1 conditions to be maintained because supply temperatures were well below the lower temperature limit of ASHRAE class 1. Predictable temperatures at the intake of the IT equipment were maintained, even when supplying only 6% more airflow rate at an air temperature of 68°F (20°C). The containment methods to physically separate the cool supply from the hot exhaust air almost completely reduced over-provisioning and bypass cool air. Increased plant efficiency was possible by raising the setpoint temperature for airflow supply without concerns of hot spots.

Well distributed airflow through floor tiles is attributed to CRAC fan control using VFD to maintain a consistent subfloor pressure, and more work is required to balance all rows and sections within the high density area to achieve near-unity balance. The air temperature at the intake grills of the IT equipment was very consistent due to supply air temperature control and all return air/heat being contained and directed back to the CRACs. Intake temperatures ranged between the supply temperatures of 68°F (20°C) and did not exceed the ASHRAE class 1 upper temperature limit of 77°F (25°C). Consistently warmer temperatures at lower rack intake positions were attributed to warm air from under racks entrainment into cool supply air due to Venturi effects caused by high velocity airstream through floor grates; a metal skirt could be used to block the forward flow of warm air.

Pressure within the rack area behind the IT equipment is critical, with acceptability of rack pressures dependent on the IT equipment installed in the rack. Control of the rack airflow rate using an automatic fan speed controller may provide the most effective operation.

This hot-air containment system provides the necessary environmental conditions for higher density IT equipment, while significantly improving energy efficiency. The total cooling delivered was closely matched to total cooling requirements for the area and is critical for effective performance to optimize energy costs. Reducing oversupply and providing higher supply air temperature allowed significant energy-saving improvements to CRAC and chiller operation. For those considering a waterside or air-side economizer, additional hours of free cooling would be available, justifying the capital expense of the economizer system, even in the most humid regions of the US.

REFERENCES

ASHRAE. 2005. *Design Considerations for Datacom Equipment Centers.* Atlanta: American Society of Heating, Refrigerating, and Air-Conditioning Engineers, Inc.

3

Non-Raised-Access Floor Case Studies

3.1 NON-RAISED-ACCESS FLOOR WITH ROW COOLING

3.1.1 CASE STUDY 10—CEDARS-SINAI MEDICAL CENTER DATA CENTER

Cedars-Sinai information technology staff were given the daunting challenge of creating a high density super computing cluster within an area of approximately 600 ft^2 (56.1 m^2). This data center supports the Spielberg Family Center for Applied Proteomics at Cedars-Sinai Medical Center in its research efforts to analyze protein profiles from blood to help doctors determine the most effective treatment protocols for patients.

This room was designed using InRow^{TM} cooling units located between the racks. These half-wide rack cooling units (RCs) have a back-to-front airflow pattern and draw warm air directly from the hot aisles and discharge cool air into the cold aisles, feeding the IT equipment in the racks. Using this configuration, high efficiency can be attained due to the high return air temperatures and short distance between the IT load and cooling units. In traditional perimeter cooling of data centers, IT exhaust air must travel relatively long distances between the racks and cooling units, adding to fan power and increasing mixing of supply and return airstreams. This reduces the return air temperature, which, in turn reduces cooling unit capacity and efficiency.

LAYOUT OF DATA CENTER

The computational engine behind this super computing center is a cluster of 370 Sun Fire X2100 single U servers, each with a base power supply of 300 W. Additional IT equipment includes SAN and networking switches. The theoretical total IT design load for the room, based upon nameplate data, is 146 kW. Additionally the room has 13 fluorescent lighting fixtures for an additional 900 W, approximately.

The converted space was formerly a concrete floor lab area. The goal was to obtain approximately 240 W/ft^2 (22.3 W/m^2) of "white space" without having to install a raised-access floor. Additionally, as seen in Figure 3.1, the room is compact and irregularly shape, further complicating the layout of IT and cooling equipment.

While conventional raised-access floor perimeter CRACs were considered, the room shape and power density made it impractical to achieve the desired cooling and redundancy levels using a traditional legacy approach.

The Cedar-Sinai Data Center can be broken down into six rack categories: server, console, storage, networking, cooling, and power. The total solution is composed of 26 equivalent rack positions, two of which are wide racks for the PDUs, each serving zones 1 and 2.

Rack quantity breakdown by type (see Table 3.1):

- (10) racks servers (37 Sun Fire single U servers each)
- (5) racks storage
- (1) racks networking (2 Catalyst 6500E switches)
- (1) racks console
- (2) wide racks PDU (APC PD80G6FK1-M)
- (2) racks UPS (APC PD80G6FK1)
- (2) racks battery (APC p/o UPS)
- (6) half-racks cooling (APC ACRC100) (equivalent of three standard racks)

The final as-built layout created one area of particular interest. The integrity of the cold aisle in zone 1, upper-right corner of Figure 3.1, is influenced directly by warm air exhausted from rack 15 containing two network switches. Racks 16, 17, and 18 were oriented with the fronts of the racks pulling air from the cold aisle. However, these racks exhaust air against a wall with a return air path across the top of the cold aisle of zone 1 before returning to a common hot aisle. Consequently, zone 1 has been divided into two cooling groups: RC1–3 and RC4–7. The control architecture is such that the RCs within a given group operate at a synchronized fan speed while independently maintaining their own supply air temperature. This allows RC1–3 to deal with local thermal challenges without penalizing the efficiency of the four other RCs in zone 1. The four other RCs (RC4–7) would have little, if any, beneficial effect on the area of interest even if their fans were operating at the higher synchronized speeds of RC1–3.

MEASUREMENT TOOLS

Field measurements were taken to evaluate the overall health of the data center and effectiveness of the implemented cooling solutions. These measurements used both native capability of the installed equipment along with temporary equipment for the purpose of measurement and data gathering.

- Velocity measurement—Kestrel 4000
- Temperature probes—Precon 10K Ω, 77°F (25°C) RTDs (60x)

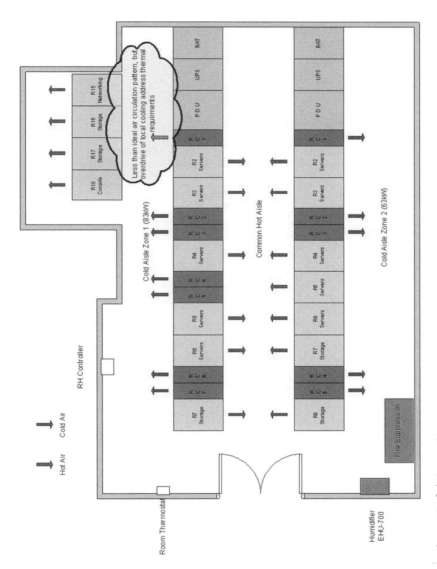

Figure 3.1 Layout of data center room.

Table 3.1   Installed Equipment Loads Name Plate vs. Actual

Type of Load	Nameplate Watts, W	Actual Watts, W	% of Nameplate, %
Servers (QTY 370)	111,000	44,445[1]	40
Storage/networking	35,000	14,015[1]	40
Lighting	900	9,00	100
UPS losses	11,130[2]	5348[3]	48
Cooling InRow™ units	12,240	3040	25
Total	**170,270**	**67,748**	**40**

1. Actual watts are based on sum of real-time PDU power (zones 1 and 2) minus unknown. InRow cooling power, and proportioned based on name plate information between servers and storage networking.
2. UPS losses are based on 92% efficiency with two 80 kW UPSs loaded to 80%.
3. UPS losses are based on 92% efficiency at actual load conditions.

- Data logger—Agilent 34970-A
- Multiplexing cards—Agilent 34910-A, 20 Channels (3x)

MEASUREMENT METHODOLOGY AND RESULTS

Airflow Measurements

Each rack type for IT equipment was traversed at 30 points. The average velocity was multiplied by the flow area to establish airflow rates. Racks of similar configuration were assumed to have more-or-less equivalent airflow (see Table 3.2).

Temperature Measurements

Along the line of vertical symmetry, temperature measurements were taken of each rack at three vertical heights on both inlet and outlet. Measurement elevations are shown in Figure 3.2. Temperatures were logged for a period of five minutes and the average value was computed for each sensor position. Additionally, temperature measurements were taken of each RC at the same elevation as the racks on both the inlet and outlet. Given the limited number of temperature sensors and data acquisition channels, it was not possible to take all of the readings concurrently. However, the RC temperatures for a given zone were taken concurrently with adjacent racks for both hot aisle and cold aisle.

Figures 3.3–3.4 represent the data captured during this period for the cold aisle side of the racks. Each rack position and RC is depicted with upper, middle, lower, and average temperature values. None of the observed temperatures at rack inlets exceed the ASHRAE (2004) recommended limit of 77°F (25°C). The average rack inlet air temperature for all measurements of zone 1 was 66.6°F (19.2°C), with a

Table 3.2 Rack Flow Table

Equipment	Zone 1		Zone 2	
	cfm	m^3/h	cfm	m^3/h
Rack 2 servers	640	1088	640	1088
Rack 3 servers	640	1088	640	1088
Rack 4 servers	640	1088	640	1088
Rack 5 servers	640	1088	640	1088
Rack 6 servers	640	1088	640	1088
Rack 7 storage	234	398	234	398
Rack 8 storage	—	—	820	1393
Rack 15 network	1600	2719	—	—
Rack 16 storage	—	—	—	—
Rack 17 storage	640	1088	—	—
Rack 18 console	—	—	—	—
Total	**5674**	**9646**	**4254**	**7232**

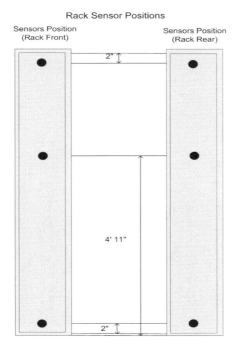

Figure 3.2 Temperature elevations.

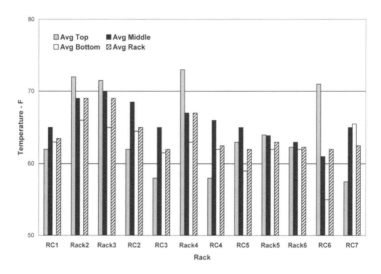

Figure 3.3 Zone 1 temperatures.

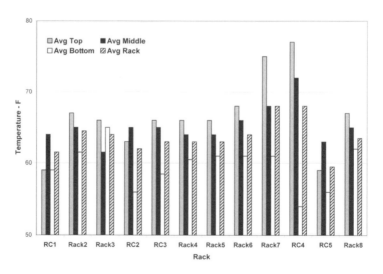

Figure 3.4 Zone 2 temperatures.

standard deviation between sensors of 3.5°F (1.9°C). The average rack inlet air temperature for all measurements of zone 2 was 65.2°F (18.4°C), with a standard deviation between sensors of 3.6°F (2.0°C).

CFD Analysis

A CFD study of the data center was used to further analyze the area of interest where hot air from racks 16, 17, and 18 circulates above the cold aisle of zone 1 before entering into the common hot aisle. Figure 3.5 clearly depicts a finger-like shape of warm air extending out and over the cold aisle for zone 1. The volumes indicated by the areas shaded in orange reflect areas with temperatures equal to or exceeding 75°F (23.9°C). The CFD was base on measured airflow and power levels recorded during the site survey along with the as-built geometry of the space.

The CFD clearly shows the temperature at rack inlet faces to be below the 75°F (23.9°C) thresholds.

Computed average rack inlet temperatures compare well with the average values measured for each rack based on the three temperature measurements taken at the specified heights (see Tables 3.3–3.4). The combined average error between the CFD and average of all actual inlet temperatures measured is only 0.4°F (0.22°C). While the scope of the case study is not to validate CFD as a tool, the degree of correlation speaks well for the overall accuracy of data recorded.

Airflows for the three groupings of RCs are shown in Table 3.5. These values reflect real-time measurements taken concurrently with temperature and load data.

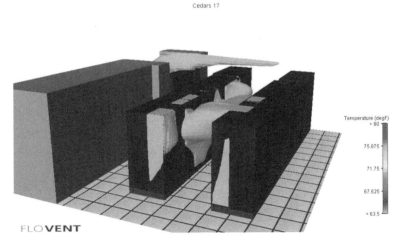

Figure 3.5 CFD warm air pockets.

Table 3.3 Zone 1 Temperature Comparison CFD vs. Actual

Average Temp.	Rack 2, °F (°C)	Rack 3, °F (°C)	Rack 4, °F (°C)	Rack 5, °F (°C)	Rack 6, °F (°C)	Rack 7, °F (°C)
CFD	64.0 (17.8)	64.5 (18.1)	64.5 (18.1)	64.0 (17.8)	64.4 (18.0)	64.0 (17.8)
Actual	63.7 (17.6)	69.3 (20.7)	67.3 (19.6)	62.6 (17.0)	63.1 (17.3)	N/A
Difference	–0.3 (0.2)	4.8 (2.6)	2.8 (1.5)	–1.4 (–0.8)	–1.3 (–0.7)	N/A

Table 3.4 Zone 2 Temperature Comparison CFD vs. Actual

Average Temp.	Rack 2, °F (°C)	Rack 3, °F (°C)	Rack4, °F (°C)	Rack 5, °F (°C)	Rack 6, °F (°C)	Rack 7, °F (°C)	Rack 8 °F (°C)
CFD	66.5 (19.2)	66.3 (19.1)	64.6 (18.1)	64.5 (18.1)	64.4 (18.0)	64.4 (18.0)	64.5 (18.1)
Actual	64.8 (18.2)	64.9 (18.3)	63.8 (17.7)	64.2 (17.9)	64.2 (17.9)	68.2 (20.1)	65.2 (18.4)
Diff.	–1.7 (–1.0)	–1.4 (–0.8)	–0.8 (–0.4)	–0.3 (–0.2)	–0.2 (–0.1)	3.8 (2.1)	0.7 (0.3)

Table 3.5 RC Group Operational Airflow

Groupings	Airflow cfm, m³/h	% Full Speed, %	CW Valve Position, %
Zone 1 (RCs 1–3)	2660 (4522)	92%	46%
Zone 1 (RCs 4–7)	1340 (2278)	46%	31%
Zone 2 (all RCs)	1290 (2193)	44%	33%

The data show the majority of RCs operating at only 44% to 46% full airflow while supporting an average rack inlet temperature of only 65°F (18.3°C). There is significant reserve in operating fan speed, chilled-water flow through the coil, and temperature to allow for increased loading and or redundancy considerations.

Energy Balance

The instrumentation and equipment installed in the room allowed for three separate assessments of load: electrical, water-side cooling, and air-side cooling (see Table 3.6). Given the nature of measurements and equipment used for monitoring, some degree of error was expected among the three sources. However, it was surprising that the air-to-electrical reconciled more favorably than the electrical-to-water. The water-side number may be biased slightly higher due to modest latent loads in the conditioned space.

It should be noted that the thermal exchange value between the conditioned room and adjacent spaces is unknowable. Observation made during the data gathering

Table 3.6   Energy Balance of Conditioned Space (kW)

Load Type	Electrical	Water Side	Air Side
PDU zone 1	34.6	N/A	N/A
PDU zone 2	26.9	N/A	N/A
UPS losses, est.	6.8	N/A	N/A
Lighting	0.9	N/A	N/A
A/C zone 1	N/A	25.1	19.4
A/C zone 2	N/A	52.6	51.2
Total	**69.2**	**77.7**	**70.6**
Energy balance vs. electrical	N/A	11.6%	2.0%

suggest that there should be a net energy gain through the walls, as surrounding areas were generally observed to be warmer than the conditioned space.

SUMMARY

This data center adheres well to ASHRAE thermal performance guidelines (ASHRAE 2004). Additionally, the total fan power of the cooling system is only 3 kW compared to the net sensible load of 66 kW. Were this room built using a conventional perimeter CRAC with similar full capacity and redundancy, it would have required an estimated fan power of 18 kW versus 3 kW (assuming fixed airflow, online N+1 redundancy, 0.3 in. (75 Pa) floor pressurization, and 72°F [22.2°C] return air).

The choice of 65°F (18.3°C) for both the supply air temperature and rack inlet temperature settings is less than optimal. Additional energy gains could easily be realized by increasing the supply air setting to 68°F (20°C) and rack inlet temperature to 72°F (22.2°C). This would allow a lower global air ratio (total cooling airflow/total IT equipment airflow), resulting in an additional fan power reduction. Rack inlet temperatures of 65°F (18.3°C) are not necessary to ensure reliable operation of the IT equipment.

The particular row-level cooling products used allow group coordination of up to 12 individual units into one synchronized group. This particular case only required a total of 11 InRow coolers but, theoretically, they all could have been combined into one large group. Avoiding this single large group approach is ideal in cases that do not allow each unit within the group to substantially contribute to the cooling of all racks targeted by the group. This particular deployment subdivided zone 1 into two specific groups along with a single group for zone 2. It is clear from the layout in Figure 3.1 that thermal requirements in zone 1 for RCs 1–3 could not have been substantially supported by the other four RCs in this zone. The decision to subdivide this zone into two groups prevents the operation of RCs 4–7 at fan speeds above the needs of their targeted racks.

Positioning the row coolers at the end of rows is ideal and prevents undesirable recirculation of the CRAC air. This placement also ensures a higher capture index for the CRACs and, thereby, a lower global air ratio (VanGilder 2007).

The cooling equipment matches well to the theoretical IT load with N+1 redundancy. This favorable gross capacity match is further aided by the dynamic fan response provided by the particular cooling product chosen. This allows for a very close match between cooling airflow and IT airflow, greatly reducing electrical demand created by cooling equipment fans.

REFERENCES

ASHRAE. 2004. *Thermal Guidelines for Data Processing Environments.* Atlanta: American Society of Heating, Refrigerating and Air-Conditioning Engineers, Inc.

VanGilder, J.W. 2007. Capture index: An airflow-based rack cooling performance metric. *ASHARE Transactions* 113(1):126–36.

3.2   NON-RAISED-ACCESS FLOOR WITH CEILING SUPPLY

3.2.1   CASE STUDY 11—LAWRENCE BERKELEY NATIONAL LAB

Rumsey Engineers and the Lawrence Berkeley National Laboratory (LBNL) conducted an energy study as part of LBNL's Data Center Load Characterization and Roadmap Project under sponsorship of the California Energy Commission. This case study documents the findings of this study, termed *Facility 6*. Additional case studies and benchmark results will be provided on LBNL's Web site (http://hightech.lbl.gov/datacenters/) as they become available. Although the format and measured data presented here are different from the other case studies in this book, the valuable data for these two centers provide additional best practices for non-raised-floor cases.

Facility 6 contains two data centers in two separate office buildings. These data centers mainly house server-type computers and data storage devices and resemble typical server farms ubiquitous in the Internet Age.[1] This percentage is relatively small; therefore, the end-use electricity of the whole building was not evaluated. Data centers 6.1 and 6.2 were 2400 ft^2 (223 m^2) and 2500 ft^2 (232 m^2), respectively. Both data centers were primarily cooled by chilled-water feeding CRACs (data center 6.1) or fan-coil units (FCUs) (data center 6.2). Both data centers were conditioned with overhead supply air and did not utilize raised floors.

The measured computer loads are listed in Table 3.7. A qualitative estimate of the rack's capacity and percent "occupied" was made, and the future computer energy loads were estimated based on this loading.

This case study describes the measurement methodology and results obtained. The study consisted of two data centers, which were measured independently. In each data center, electricity end use was determined. This means that the energy consumed by all equipment related to the data center was measured. Such equipment includes the actual computer power consumption, the data center air-conditioning equipment, the lighting, and the losses associated with the UPS. The computer load density is determined based on the gross area of the data center. This number, in watts per square foot (W/ft^2) is the metric typically used by facility engineers to represent the power density.

Table 3.7   Current and Future Computer Loads

Data Center	Data Center Area, ft^2	Comp. Load, kW	Comp. Load Energy Density, W/ft^2	Occupancy, %	Projected Comp. Load Energy Density, W/ft^2	# of Racks	kW/ Rack
6.1	2400	155	65	80%	81	101	1.5
6.2	2501	119	48	50%	95	83	1.4

1. Based on rack configuration, high density of computers, and the absence of large mainframe servers common in older data centers.

Based on a qualitative observation of the data center occupancy, the computer load density at full occupancy is extrapolated. In addition to the typical W/ft^2 metric, the density is also calculated based on the number of racks and the rack footprint.

Additional information was collected so that the efficiencies of the cooling equipment could be calculated. These efficiencies are compared to the design efficiencies. Opportunities for energy-efficiency improvements are described, which are based on observation of the mechanical system design and measured performance. General design guidance is presented for consideration in future construction. Data center specific recommendations are made for the as-built systems.

Site Overview

Facility 6 is located in Silicon Valley in California. Two data centers were monitored for energy consumption at Facility 6. The data centers are in separate office buildings and constitute a relatively small percentage of the total building area (less than 10%). The data centers are 2400 ft^2 (223 m^2) and 2500 ft^2 (232 m^2), respectively. Since the data centers represent a small percentage of the overall building area, whole-building power consumption is not relevant to determining the data centers' power consumption and was not monitored. Both data centers house servers and storage drives and operate 24 hours a day. Data center 6.1 serves corporate needs, while data center 6.2 is mainly used for research and development of new engineering products. Occasionally, during normal business hours, a small number of employees may be in the data centers working with the computers (see Figure 3.6).

Figure 3.6   IT equipment.

ENERGY USE—DATA CENTER 6.1

Electrical Equipment and Backup Power System

The facility utilizes a balanced power 225 kVA UPS to provide a constant supply of power to the data center at constant delivery voltage (480/277 V). The UPS converts and stores alternating current as direct current in multiple battery packs. To power the IT equipment, power is converted back to alternating current. In the event of a power loss, a 400 kW diesel generator provides power for approximately ten hours.

Spot power measurements were taken at the UPS, at both the input and output, to determine computer plug loads and losses at the UPS system (see Table 3.8).

Cooling System

The data center is cooled separately from the remainder of the building by a chilled-water system. The system consists of two Trane air-cooled chillers, a 40 ton scroll chiller, and a 100 ton rotary chiller. The nominal efficiencies of the chillers are 1.1 and 1.3 kW/ton, respectively.[1] The 100 ton chiller is served by the emergency distribution panel (EDP) and is the primary chiller, though the 40 ton chiller is often run in unison to ensure a sufficient supply of chilled water. The chilled-water pumps are 1.5 hp (hydraulic horsepower; brake horsepower unlisted) variable-speed pumps with control based on a differential pressure setpoint. A controlled bypass ensures minimum flow through the chillers. The chilled-water system branches off into two feeds, one which is dedicated to the data center, and the other which feeds the computer labs.

Table 3.8   UPS Electrical Measurements

UPS Property	Electrical Use[1]
UPS input	164.73 kW
UPS output	154.9 kW
UPS losses	9.83 kW
UPS efficiency	94%

1. Average measurements taken on August 21, 2002, using the PowerSight power meter.

1. Converted from the energy efficiency ratio (EER) listed on the equipment schedules. The schedule for the 100 ton chiller was incomplete and, therefore, its EER was assumed to be the same as the identical model chillers that are installed for data center 6.2. The nominal loads are based on entering evaporator water temperature of 56°F, leaving evaporator water temperature of 44°F, entering condenser air temperature of 95°F, and flow rates of 80 gpm and 200 gpm.

Power consumption, flow, and chilled-water temperatures[1] were measured at each chiller over a period of several days to determine the chiller efficiency over a period of varying temperatures.

The CRACs are constant-speed air-handling units (AHUs) that are supplied chilled water (see Figure 3.7). There are three air handlers in total with total cooling capacities of 286,900, 551,700, and 185,400 Btu/h, respectively, and design airflows of 9200, 12,700, and 8000 cfm (260.5, 359.6, and 226.5 m³/min), respectively.[2] Air is returned through grills in the front of the AHU and exits from the top to ducts that feed the ceiling diffusers. The AHUs control the return air temperature to 70°F (21.1°C). In addition to the air that is recirculated and cooled by the AHUs, ventilation air is supplied by the main building air-conditioning unit. The air handlers do not have humidity control.

Figure 3.7 Data center AHU.

1. These were measured using an Elite power measuring instrument, an ultrasonic flow meter for pipe flow, and thermistors inserted in the Pete's plugs at the inlet and outlet of the chilled-water line.
2. The numbering refers to the numbering physically on the units. (CRU #1, CRU #2, CRU #3). This does not correspond with the numbering on the equipment schedule based on the anticipated motor kW.

Spot measurements of flow and temperatures were performed at the AHU chilled-water supply lines.[1] In addition, flow rate and supply and return chilled-water temperatures to all three handlers were monitored over a period of several days.[2] It was necessary to identify the chilled water supplied solely to the data center in order to segregate the chiller power consumption due to cooling of the data center only. Spot measurements of airflow through the AHUs were measured along with the AHU power consumption to determine how efficiently air is moved.[3]

The spot measurements and average of trended measurements are listed in the Table 3.9. The chiller pump and chiller power are proportioned to the data center cooling load in order to properly determine electrical end use for the data center.

Lighting

Lighting in the data center consists of T-8 tubular fluorescent lamps. All lights were on when taking power measurements.

Lighting Power: 1.16 kW (taken on 8/21/02) or 0.5 W/ft^2.

Summary Measurements and Metrics

Table 3.10 summarizes the equipment electrical measurements for the data center, and the results are shown graphically in Figure 3.8.

The computer loads, based on readings at the UPS power supply, amount to 74% of the data center energy usage. Pumping and cooling energy is the second largest consumer at 16%, and air movement is 5%. Together, the HVAC component amounts to 21% of data center energy use—a significant amount. Therefore, efficiency improvements in energy for HVAC could be significant. Losses in the UPS account for 5% of the data center energy consumption. These losses are more than the lighting, which amount to only 1% of total energy use.

The electrical and cooling loads can be represented by different metrics. The most commonly used metric among mission-critical facilities is the computer load density in watts consumed per square foot. However, the square footage is not always consistent from one designer to the next. Some data centers use kVA/rack or kW/rack as a design parameter. The definition of *data center floor area* includes the gross area of the data center, which includes rack spaces, aisle spaces, and areas that may eventually contain computer equipment. Per the Uptime Institute definition of an

---

1. These measurements were taken by measuring pressure drop across the circuit setter on the chilled water line and by measuring temperatures at Pete's Plugs on the supply and return lines.
2. These measurements were made at the main branch that feeds only these units. Chilled-water temperatures were performed by inserting thermistor probes between insulation and the pipe surface. Flow measurements were made using an ultrasonic flowmeter.
3. Airflow was taken by multiplying the average velocity across the return grille with the grille area, where the velocity was taken with a Shortridge velocity grid.

Table 3.9 Cooling Equipment Electrical and Load Measurements

Equipment	Spot/Monitored	Date	Measurement	Units
Chiller pumps—total	Spot	8/21/02	3.97	kW
Chiller pumps—proportioned Based on data center load	Spot	8/21/02	1.99	kW
AHU 1 (compuaire C)[8]	Spot	8/21/02	3.72	kW
AHU 2 (compuaire B)[9]	Spot	8/21/02	4.72	kW
AHU 3 (compuaire A)[10]	Spot	8/21/02	1.75	kW
AHU 1 Tonnage	Spot	8/21/02	12	tons
AHU 2 tonnage	Spot	8/21/02	16	tons
AHU 3 tonnage	Spot	8/21/02	7	tons
AHU 1 airflow	Spot	9/4/02	5086	cfm
AHU 2 airflow	Spot	9/4/02	6494	cfm
AHU 3 airflow	Spot	8/21/02	2432	cfm
DC cooling load from chilled water— Based on AHU tonnage	Spot	8/21/02	124	kW
DC cooling load from chilled water— from monitoring of chilled-water use	Monitored	8/30/02– 9/4/02	111	kW
Chiller 1 (40 ton)	Spot	8/21/02	16	kW
Chiller 2 total (100 ton)	Spot	8/21/02	48	kW
DC chiller power from spots[1]	Spot	8/21/02	35.37	kW
DC chiller power from monitoring—average	Monitored	8/30/02– 9/4/02	32.34	kW

1. Individual chiller kW proportioned based on the data center cooling load versus total chiller load. This value will vary when the chiller load changes, even if the data center load stays constant, as the efficiency of the chiller is not constant.

Table 3.10   Summary of Electrical Measurements

Equipment Loads	Power, kW	Percent of Total, %
Computer loads	154.90	74%
UPS losses	9.83	5%
HVAC—air movement	10.00	5%
HVAC—pumps and chiller	34.00	16%
Lighting	1.16	1%
Total Energy Use	**209.89**	**100%**

Energy Balance - Data Center - Facility 6. Data Center 6.1

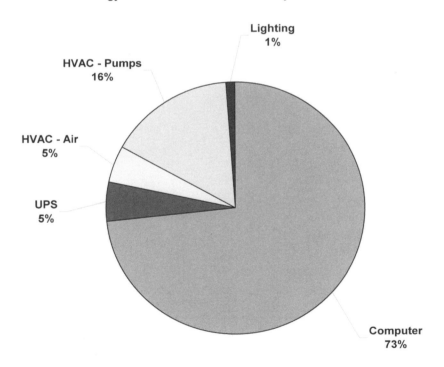

Figure 3.8   Energy usage of data center 6.1.

electrically active floor area, the resulting computer load density in W/ft^2 is consistent with what facility engineers use, though this is different from the "footprint" energy density that manufacturers use. We have also calculated the W/ft^2 based on the rack area alone. In addition to the previous metrics, the noncomputer energy densities are calculated, based on the data center area. Using the data center occupancy,[1] the computer load density at 100% occupancy is projected (see Table 3.11).

The computer load density based on the data center area (gross area) is 65 W/ft^2 (699.6 W/m^2). At full occupancy, the computer load density is projected to be 81 W/ft^2 (871.9 W/m^2). The computer load density based on *rack area* is presently 246 W/ft^2 (2647.9 W/m^2) and is projected to be 307 W/ft^2 (3305 W/m^2) at full occupancy. The average computer load based on the number of racks is currently 1.3 kW/rack and is projected to be 1.6 kW/rack at full capacity. The noncomputer energy density, which includes HVAC, lighting, and UPS losses, is measured at 23 W/ft^2 (247.6 W/m^2).

Since the rack density within data centers and computer types are site specific, a more useful metric for evaluating how efficiently the data center is cooled can be represented as a ratio of cooling power to computer power. The *theoretical cooling*

Table 3.11   Electrical Consumption Metrics

	Measurement	Units
Data center gross area[1]	2400	ft^2
Rack area	630	ft^2 (Calculated from a total of 121 racks and area of 1 rack)
"Occupied"%	80%	Estimated from visual inspection
Based on Gross Area		
Computer load density	65	W/ft^2
Non-computer load density	23	W/ft^2
Project computer load density	81	W/ft^2
Based on Rack Area[2]		
Computer load density	246	W/ft^2
Project computer load density	307	W/ft^2
On an Individual Rack Basis[3]		
Computer load density	1.3	kW/rack
Project computer load density	1.6	kW/rack

1. Gross area includes spaces between racks; does not include entire building area.
2. This is an important metric, because the data center gross area can vary depending on spacing between racks.
3. This is the average rack computer load.

1. A qualitative assessment of how physically full the data center is. In this facility, occupancy was determined by a visual inspection of how full the racks in place were.

load is the same as the sum of the computer loads and lighting loads (together, the plug loads). (There is a small amount of human activity; however, the energy load is insignificant compared to the computer loads.) This is a good cross check of measurements and may also be an indication of the level of cooling that is provided by non-data-center-dedicated cooling equipment (i.e., general office building or "house" air to achieve minimum ventilation). The more traditional metrics of energy per ton of cooling (kW/ton) are calculated for total HVAC efficiency (chillers, pumps, and air handlers) and for the chillers. The air-handler efficiency is based on how much air is actually being moved for the measured power consumption.

Table 3.12 shows that the cooling efficiency is 0.3 kW/kW. This, however, is based on a cooling load that is below the theoretical cooling load by 30%, which suggests that significant cooling is achieved by the whole-building cooling system (package units). The efficiency and operation of this system was not evaluated. However, the whole-building system has the ability to provide cooling by supplying outdoor air when the weather is favorable (i.e., economizing), a very efficient way to provide cooling.

The average chiller efficiencies are slightly better than the design efficiencies, which are at ARI conditions. This is expected since the ARI conditions assume 95°F (35°C) air temperature entering the condenser, which is higher than the average

Table 3.12   HVAC Efficiency Metrics

Metric	Value	Units
Cooling kW: Computer load kW	0.3	—
Theoretical cooling load[1]	47	tons
Cooling provided by AHUs and chilled water	32	tons
Cooling Provided by House Air (Based on Energy Balance)	13	tons
Combined chiller efficiency	1.0	kW/ton
Average chiller 1 (40 ton) efficiency	0.9	kW/ton
Chiller 1 design efficiency	1.1	kW/ton
Average chiller 2 (100 ton) efficiency	1.0	kW/ton
Chiller 2 design efficiency	1.3	kW/ton
Overall HVAC efficiency	1.3	kW/ton
AHU 1 efficiency—measured	1367	CFM/kW
AHU 2 efficiency—measured	1375	CFM/kW
AHU 3 efficiency—measured	1387	CFM/kW
AHU 1 design efficiency	2221	CFM/kW
AHU 2 design efficiency	2044	CFM/kW
AHU 3 design efficiency	3219	CFM/kW

1. Based on computer loads, lighting loads, and fan energy.

temperatures experienced during the monitored period. When outdoor air temperatures are below this temperature, the chiller can reject energy more easily, and therefore has lower power consumption. Based on the outdoor air conditions in this area, better efficiencies are expected. For every 1°F (0.6°C) drop in condenser temperature (outdoor air temperature), the chiller should experience an approximate 2.5% increase in efficiency. In addition, their performance is poor compared to the performance of typical water-cooled chillers. This area is certainly an area of opportunity for energy savings in future construction.

The air-handler airflow delivery efficiencies were measured at 1367, 1375, and 1387 cfm/kW, which are below the design efficiencies by 40%–60%. This is likely caused by increased pressure drop in the existing ductwork, which results in a decrease in airflow, compared to the standard conditions under which fans are tested. Low pressure drop duct design is important for achieving high air movement efficiencies.

ENERGY USE—DATA CENTER 6.2

Electrical Equipment and Backup Power System

The facility utilizes an International Power Machine 160kVA UPS (UPS1), and a Chloride 50 Power Electronics 50kVA UPS (UPS2) to provide a constant supply of power of constant delivery voltage (480 V) to the data center (see Table 3.13). The UPS converts alternating current and stores it as direct current in multiple battery packs. When the voltage is needed, it is converted back to alternating current. In the

Table 3.13   UPS Electrical Measurements

UPS Property	Electrical Use[1]
UPS 1	
UPS Input	103.55 kW
UPS Output	96.27 kW
UPS Losses	7.28 kW
UPS Efficiency	93%
UPS 2	
UPS Input	25.43 kW
UPS Output	22.83 kW
UPS Losses	2.60 kW
UPS Efficiency	90%

1. Average measurements taken August 27–28, 2002.

event of a power loss, a 750 kW diesel generator provides power for approximately ten hours.

Spot power measurements were taken at the UPS at both the input and output in order to determine computer plug loads as well as losses at the UPS system.

Note, the UPS efficiencies at data center 6.2 are slightly higher than the efficiency measured for the UPS serving data center 6.1.

Cooling System

The data center is cooled by a chilled-water system that consists of two 220 ton Trane rotary air-cooled chillers. The nominal efficiencies of the chillers are 1.3 kW/ton.[1] The chillers are piped in parallel, and both typically operate at all times. The EDP serves one of the chillers. The chilled-water pumps are 8.5 hp (hydraulic horsepower) constant speed pumps. One main pipe feeds the cooling loads on each floor; however, the data center is the last load fed by the main pipe.

As with data center 6.1, power consumption, flow, and chilled-water temperatures[2] were measured at each chiller over a period of several days to determine the chiller efficiency over a period of varying temperatures.

Unlike the other data center, the chilled water feeds FCUs in the ceiling plenum, which supplies the overhead duct system. The FCUs are constant speed and have three-way valves. The system consists of a total of seven FCUs with cooling capacities ranging from 104,000–190,000 Btu/h (30.5–55.7 kW) and design airflow ranging from 5300–9600 cfm (271.8–150 m³/min). Air is returned through grills in the ceiling. Minimum outdoor air is brought in through the house air-conditioning system. As with data center 6.1, there is no humidity control in data center 6.2.

The total chilled-water load to all the FCUs was monitored using the technique of measuring flow rate and pipe surface temperatures.[3] As with the previous data center, it was necessary to identify the load solely to the data center in order to segregate the chiller power consumption due to cooling of the data center only. The number and arrangement of the FCUs did not allow for measurement of individual fan-coil cooling load or air-supply flow rate.

The spot measurements and average of trended measurements are listed in Table 3.14 below. The chiller pump and chiller power are proportioned to the data center cooling load in order to properly determine the electrical end use in the data center.

---

1. Based on 420 gpm, entering and leaving chilled-water temperatures of 56°F and 44°F, respectively, and an entering condenser-water temperature of 95°F.
2. These were measured using an Elite power measuring instrument, an ultrasonic flowmeter for pipe flow, and thermistors inserted in the Pete's plugs at the inlet and outlet of the chilled-water line.
3. These measurements were made at the main branch that feeds only these units. Chilled-water temperatures were performed by inserting thermistor probes between insulation and the pipe surface. Flow measurements were made using an ultrasonic flowmeter.

Table 3.14   Cooling Equipment Electrical and Load Measurements

Equipment	Spot/ Monitored	Date	Measurement, kW
Chiller pumps—total	Spot	9/4/02	23.52
Chiller pumps— Proportioned based on data center load	Spot	9/4/02	4.00
Fan-coils (on circuits 23, 25, 27)	Spot	9/4/02	5.56
Fan-coils (on circuits 29, 31, 33)	Spot	9/4/02	2.50
Fan-coils (on circuits 35, 37, 39)	Spot	9/4/02	11.83
DC cooling load from chilled water— from monitoring of chilled-water use	Monitored	8/27/02–9/4/02	158
DC chiller power from monitoring— average	Monitored	8/27/02–9/4/02	45.9

Lighting

Lighting in the data center consists of T-8 tubular fluorescent lamps, and all lights were on when taking power measurements.

Lighting power: 2.65 kW (measured on 8/27/02) or 1.1 W/ft^2 (11.8 W/m^2). These values are more than double what was measured for data center 1.

Summary Measurements and Metrics

Table 3.15 brings together all the equipment electrical measurements for the data center, and the results are shown graphically in Figure 3.9.

The computer loads, based on the measured UPS power supply, amount to 59% of the data center energy usage. Pumping and cooling energy is the second largest consumer at 25%, and air movement from the FCUs is 10%. Together, the HVAC component amounts to a significant 35% of data center energy use. Therefore, the HVAC components provide a significant opportunity for energy savings. Losses at the UPS consume 5% of data center energy consumption. The percentage of lighting power consumption was the same for both data centers, measured at 1%, though the energy density (W/ft^2) for data center 6.2 was higher.

Commensurate with the discussion of data center 6.1, different metrics are calculated for the data center energy use and energy efficiency (see Table 3.16). To briefly reiterate, the computer load density is based on both gross area, which we equate to data center floor area, and rack floor area. Both are extrapolated to 100% occupancy to predict future loads.

The computer load density based on the data center area (gross area) is 48 W/ft^2 (516.7 W/m^2). At full occupancy, the computer load density is projected to be 95 W/ft^2

Table 3.15   Summary of Electrical Measurements

Equipment Loads	Power, kW	% of Total, %
Computer loads	119.10	59%
UPS losses	9.88	5%
HVAC—air movement	19.89	10%
HVAC—pumps and chiller	49.00	25%
Lighting	2.65	1%
Total Energy Use	**200.52**	**100%**

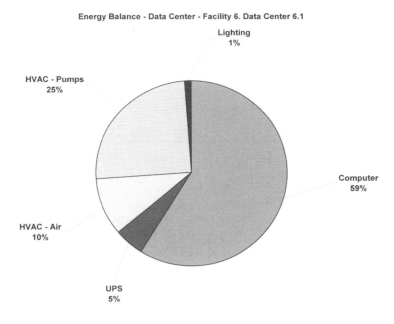

Energy Balance - Data Center - Facility 6. Data Center 6.1

Figure 3.9   Energy usage of facility 6.2.

(1022.6 W/m^2). This requires approximately 40 more tons of cooling, which based on the average measured chiller load, cannot be met by the chillers. The computer load density, based on rack area, is presently 276 W/ft^2 (2970.8 W/m^2) and is projected to be 551 W/ft^2 (5930.9 W/m^2) at full occupancy. The average computer load, based on the number of racks, is currently 1.4 kW/rack and is projected to be 2.9 kW/rack at full capacity. The non-computer energy density, which includes HVAC, lighting, and UPS losses, is measured at 33 W/ft^2.

Table 3.16   Electrical Consumption Metrics

	Measurement	Units
Data center gross area	2501	ft^2
Rack area	432	ft^2 (Calculated from a total of 83 racks and area of 1 rack)
"Occupied"%	50%	Estimated from visual inspect
Based on Gross Area		
Computer load density	48	W/ft^2
Non-computer load density	33	W/ft^2
Project computer load density	95	W/ft^2
Based on Rack Area		
Computer load density	276	W/ft^2
Project Computer load density	551	W/ft^2
On Individual Rack Basis		
Computer load density	1.4	kW/rack
Project computer load density	2.9	kW/rack

Commensurate with data center 6.1, the energy efficiency metrics for data center 6.2 are shown in Table 3.17.

Table 3.17 shows that the cooling efficiency of approximately 0.6 kW/kW is significantly less efficient than the cooling efficiency for data center 6.1. This is explained by the differences in equipment, but the comparison is entirely valid, since data center 6.1's metrics suggest that significant cooling is provided by the whole-building air-conditioning system. This does not appear to be the case with data center 6.2, where the measured cooling load is more than 10 tons larger than the theoretical cooling load.[1]

The performance of the chillers is similar to what was observed in data center 6.2 (i.e., the performance was slightly better than the ARI-rated performance, which is expected for the operating conditions). However, the performance of water-cooled chillers far outweighs the performance of these units and is an opportunity for energy savings in future construction.

The design efficiencies of the FCUs are comparable to the design efficiencies of the AHUs used in data center 6.1, although the actual efficiencies were not measured.

---

1. This is attributed to measurement error of the cooling load and the fact that computer loads were assumed to be constant, while they actually may vary a small percent over time. This assumes no other FCUs on the first floor serve non-data center rooms, which would explain the small difference.

Table 3.17   HVAC Efficiency Metrics

Metric	Value	Units
Cooling kW: Computer load kW	0.58	—
Theoretical cooling load	40	tons
Cooling provided by chilled water and FCU	44	tons
Chiller 1 design efficiency	1.0	kW/ton
Chiller 2 design efficiency	1.1	kW/ton
Chiller 1–2 design efficiency	1.3	kW/ton
Average chiller efficiency	1.0	kW/ton
FCU design efficiency	2370	cfm/kW
Overall HVAC efficiency	1.6	kW/ton

ENERGY EFFICIENCY RECOMMENDATIONS

General Guidelines for Future Construction

Efficient Chilled-Water System. Water-cooled chillers offer enormous energy savings over air-cooled chillers, particularly in dry climates, such as the San Francisco Bay area, because they take advantage of evaporative cooling. Since the chiller is cooled by lower-temperature media, it can reject heat more easily and does not have to work as hard. Though the addition of a cooling tower adds maintenance costs associated with the water treatment, we have found that the energy savings outweigh the maintenance costs. Within the options of water-cooled chillers, variable-speed centrifugal are the most energy efficient because they can operate very efficiently at low loads. Figure 3.10 compares the energy performance of various chiller types.

Though there are efficient air-cooled chillers, the larger size of water-cooled chillers has resulted in more care given to efficiency and life-cycle costs compared to air-cooled chillers.

The selection of the auxiliary equipment, including cooling towers, pumps, and pumping strategy, should also be carefully considered. For example, variable-speed fans on cooling towers allow for optimized cooling tower control. Premium-efficiency motors and high-efficiency pumps are recommended, and variable-speed pumping is a ripe opportunity for pump savings. Variable pumping strategies can be achieved in a primary/secondary scheme, where the primary pumps operate at constant speed and directly feed water to the chiller, and the secondary pumps are variable speed and serve the AHUs. A more energy-efficient scheme is a primary-only variable-speed pumping strategy. Pumping savings are based on the cube law:

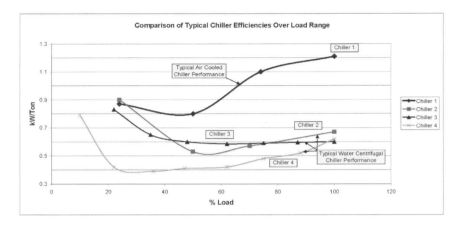

Chiller 1	250-Ton, Screw, Standard Efficiency, Air Cooled
Chiller 2	216 Ton, Screw, Water Cooled
Chiller 3	227-Ton, Centrifugal, Constant Speed, Water Cooled
Chiller 4	227-Ton, Centrifugal, Variable Speed, Water Cooled

Figure 3.10 Chiller efficiency.

pump power is reduced by the cube of the reduction in pump speed, which is directly proportional to the amount of fluid pumped.

A primary-only variable pumping strategy must include a bypass valve that ensures minimum flow to the chiller, and the use of two-way valves at the AHUs in order to achieve lower pumping speeds. The control speed of the bypass valve should also meet the chiller manufacturer's recommendations of allowable turndown, such that optimum chiller efficiency is achieved.[1] Figure 3.11 describes the primary-only variable-speed pumping strategy.

Air Management. The standard practice of cooling data centers employs an underfloor system fed by CRACs. One common challenge with underfloor supply is that the underfloor becomes congested with cabling, which increases the resistance to airflow. This results in an increase in fan energy use. A generous underfloor depth is essential for effective air distribution (we have seen 3 ft [0.9 m] in one facility).

An alternative to an underfloor air distribution system is a high-velocity overhead supply combined with ceiling height returns. Such systems can be designed efficiently if care is taken to keep air pressure drops to a minimum. In most cases,

---

1. This means that the flow through the chiller should be varied slow enough so that the chiller is able to reach a quasi-steady-state condition and able to perform to its maximum efficiency.

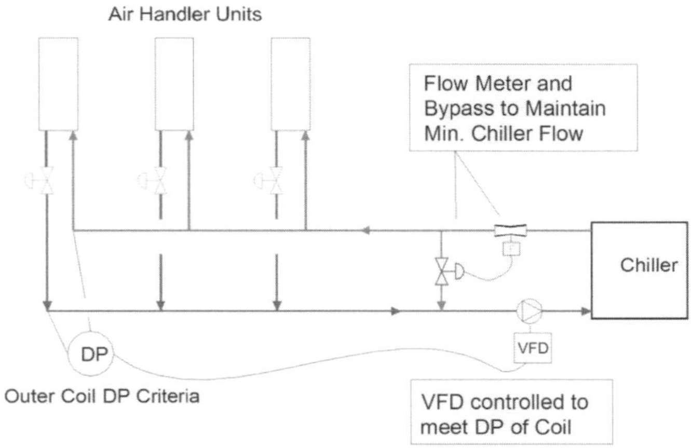

Figure 3.11 Variable-speed pumping strategy.

duct design to accommodate air-side economizers is also simpler with central air-handling systems.

Another common problem identified with CRACs is that they often fight each other in order to maintain a constant humidity setpoint. Humidity control systems should be designed to prevent such fighting; this is relatively simple with large air handlers serving a single space but can also be accomplished by controlling all CRACs in unison.

Air Management—Rack Configuration. Another factor that influences cooling in data centers is the server rack configuration. It is more logical for the aisles to be arranged so that servers' backs are facing each other and servers' fronts are facing each other. This way, cool air is drawn in through the front, and hot air blown out the back. The Uptime Institute has published documents describing this method for air management.[1] Our observations of both data centers showed an inconsistent rack configuration.

Commissioning of New Systems and Optimized Control Strategies

Many times the predicted energy savings of new and retrofit projects are not fully realized. Often, this is due to poor and/or incomplete implementation of the energy efficiency recommendations. Commissioning is the process of ensuring that the building systems perform as they were intended to in the design. Effective

1. http://www.upsite.com/TUIpages/whitepapers/tuiaisles.html.

commissioning actually begins at the design stage, where the design strategy is critically reviewed. Either the design engineer serves as the commissioning agent or a third-party commissioning agent is hired. Commissioning is different from standard start-up testing in that it ensures systems function well relative to each other. In other words, it employs a systems approach.

Many of the problems identified in building systems are often associated with controls. A good controls scheme begins at the design level. In our experience, an effective controls design includes (1) a detailed points list with accuracy levels and sensor types and (2) a detailed sequence of operations. Both of these components are essential to successfully implement the recommended high-efficiency chilled-water system described above.

Though commissioning is relatively new to the industry, various organizations have developed standards and guidelines. Such guidelines are available through organizations, such as the Portland Energy Conservation Inc. (www.peci.org) or the American Society of Heating, Refrigerating and Air-Conditioning Engineers, Inc. (*ASHRAE Guideline 1-1996* and *ASHRAE Guideline 0-2005, The Commissioning Process*).

Lighting Controls

The lighting power and lighting power densities for data center 6.2 were more than twice those of data center 6.1. This is likely a result of occupants/engineers entering the data center and turning the lights on. Lighting controls, such as occupancy sensors, may be appropriate for these types of areas that are infrequently or irregularly occupied. If 24-hour lighting is desired for security reasons, scarce lighting can be provided at all hours, with additional lighting for occupied periods.

Data Center 6.1 Specific Observations

Verification of Bypass Control. The chilled-water pumping for data center 6.1 utilizes a primary-only variable-speed drive (VSD) system with a bypass control valve. From our observation of the energy management control system (EMCS), the VSD is being controlled via a differential pressure sensor; however, the control scheme for the bypass valve is not clear. A pressure-independent bypass control is the most effective, where the actual flow supplied to the chiller is monitored and used as the control input to the bypass control valve. A pressure-dependent system maintains a constant differential pressure and controls flow by using pressure as a surrogate. The control scheme for the bypass control valve should be examined to ensure that it is being controlled properly.

Three-Way Valves and Bypass. Though primary-only variable pumping system equipment has been installed, it is not clear whether the AHUs serving the data center and FCUs serving the computer labs are equipped with two-way valves, as they should be. In order for a variable system to function as intended, the AHUs and FCUs should be equipped with two-way control valves.

Chiller Staging. Currently, both chillers are running most of the time, regardless of the load. It would be more efficient to stage the chillers so that the smaller chiller comes on when the larger chiller is unable to satisfy the cooling requirements. This staging could be based on the primary chiller being unable to meet its chilled-water setpoint. The measured data showed that the load did not exceed 90 tons and, therefore, the large chiller should be capable meeting the load most of the time. Attention should be paid to how quickly flow is diverted from the primary chiller so that it does not go off inadvertently on low load.

Triple-Duty Valves. Triple-duty valves have been installed on the discharge of each of the chilled-water pumps. It was recommended that the triple-duty valves be opened completely.

Data Center 6.2 Specific Observations

Chiller Oscillations. The measured data identified power oscillations with chiller 1. This could be due to cycling of one of the compressors. The controls of this chiller should be investigated, since this cycling effect has an adverse effect on energy consumption and increases maintenance cost. Though chiller staging is achievable for data center 6.1, the measured data shows that the chilled-water load for the building hosting data center 2 exceeds the nominal load of one chiller.

Close Four-Inch Bypass. The mechanical drawings show the existence of a 4 in. bypass on the chilled-water loop located on the first floor. Visual observation of the FCUs show the existence of three-way valves (though this differs from the mechanical drawings). Upon confirmation of three-way valves on all FCUs, this bypass can be closed.

Primary-Only Variable-Speed Conversion. The current constant-speed pumping strategy could be converted to a variable-speed system by installing VFDs on the pumps, installing a controlled bypass line to ensure minimum flow through the chillers, and converting the three-way valves to two-way valves. Note, this is the system that is already installed on the chilled-water system serving data center 6.1.

High-Velocity Diffusers and Air Management. Both data centers utilize overhead air supply. Diffusers should be sized for high velocities so that air is directed downward in aisles facing the fronts of the servers (see also, "Air Management—Rack Configuration" above).

Triple-Duty Valves. Triple-duty valves were installed on the discharge of each of the chilled-water pumps. It was recommended that the triple-duty valves be opened and that the pump impellers be trimmed for balancing. This has the same effect as reducing the pump size and flow without sacrificing efficiency. If a conversion is made to variable-speed pumping, then the impeller does not have to be trimmed.

4

Best Practices

The following information collects the best ideas in data center cooling literature over the last five years (Schmidt and Iyengar 2007), including best practices
from some of the case studies presented in this book. A review of literature prior to
2002 can be found in Schmidt and Shaukatullah (2003), and a discussion of this topic
was presented by Schmidt et al. (2005d). Belady and Beaty (2005) provide a broad
high-level framework for data center cooling roadmaps. Beaty et al. (2005a, 2005b)
present a two-part study that covers important aspects of data center cooling design,
such as load calculation, space planning, cooling-system choices, and modifying
legacy low heat flux facilities to allow for high density computer equipment clusters.
Belady and Malone (2006) report projected heat flux and rack power information for
the future to complement the work of ASHRAE (2005).

The different topics covered herein include data center new-building design,
accomodating future growth, raised-access and non-raised-access floor designs,
localized rack cooling, and energy management and efficiency.

4.1   DATA CENTER—NEW BUILDS

When building a new data center, basic cooling concepts need to be evaluated
before one selects that which best fits the needs of the IT customer and accommo-
dates future growth. With this in mind, basic questions need to be answered before
one proceeds to outline the structural requirements of a new data center.

1. Of the numerous potential ventilation schemes, which is best suited for air cool-
    ing datacom equipment?
2. If a raised-access floor is planned, what underfloor plenum height should one
    choose to allow proper distribution of airflow while being mindful of construc-
    tion costs?
3. What ceiling height is optimum for both raised-access (underfloor supply) and
    non-raised-access floor (overhead supply) data centers?

4. Where should one place cabling trays and piping under a raised-access floor to minimize airflow distribution problems?

5. How should one design for future growth and an increase in datacom equipment power, which increases cooling needs?

6. Where should CRACs be placed for most efficient use and best cooling of IT equipment?

These are basic questions that need to be answered before the planning process continues. This section attempts to outline the best thinking on these issues in the industry.

4.1.1 VENTILATION DESIGNS

Nakao et al. (1991) numerically modeled representative geometries for four data center ventilation schemes: underfloor supply (raised-access floor) with ceiling exhaust, overhead supply with underfloor exhaust, underfloor supply with horizontal exhaust, and overhead supply with horizontal exhaust. The heat flux modeled was for 61.3 W/ft^2 (660 W/m^2) with 80%–220% chilled-air supply fractions of total rack flow rate. Noh et al. (1998) used CFD modeling to compare three different designs for the data center—underfloor supply (raised-access floor) with ceiling exhaust, overhead supply with underfloor exhaust, and overhead supply with horizontal (wall) exhaust—using 5–6 kW racks that provided heat fluxes of 37.1 W/ft^2 (400 W/m^2) for telecommunications applications. Shrivastava et al. (2005a) used numerical CFD modeling to characterize and contrast the thermal performance of seven distinct ventilation schemes for data center air cooling, as illustrated in Figure 4.1. In a continuation of this work, Shrivastava et al. (2005b) used statistical significance levels to quantify the effect of three variables—ceiling height, chilled-air supply percentage, and return vent location—on the facility thermal performance for the seven designs shown in Figure 4.1. Sorell et al. (2005) also used CFD to compare the non-raised-access floor (overhead supply) design with the raised-access floor (under-floor) designs for air delivery. Herrlin and Belady (2006) and Schmidt and Iyengar (2007) have also used CFD methods to compare underfloor and overhead air supply designs, respectively.

Furihata et al. (2003, 2004a, 2004b) and Hayama et al. (2003, 2004) developed an air-conditioning flow method that reduces the volume of supplied air while maintaining proper cooling for the computer equipment, and they established an airflow adjustment mechanism design methodology for proper distribution of supplied air for air conditioning. They monitored the temperature of the exit air from racks and controlled the flow into the rack to maintain similar outlet temperatures for all the racks. This method required a flow-control mechanism be added to the bottom of the racks. Spinazzola (2003) discussed a specialized cooling configuration whereby air is ducted in and out of the rack via the intake and exhaust plenums, and the server

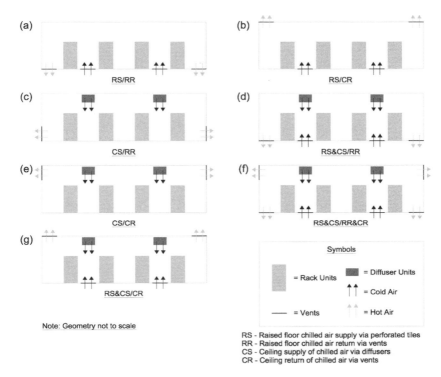

Figure 4.1 Ventilation scheme modeled (Shrivastava et al. 2005a).

equipment is designed to higher air temperature rise through the server, resulting in energy savings with respect to CRAC capacity.

Recommendations and Guidelines

- Depending on the parameters studied, some designs favor raised-access floors and others favor non-raised-access floors. Technical papers have been written that support each of these designs.

  - The best ventilation scheme uses a raised-access floor for chilled-air supply, with vents in the ceiling or top parts of the walls (see Figure 4.1b) (Noh et al. 1998; Nakao et al. 1991; Shrivastava et al. 2005a) or CRACs set on the raised-access floor (see Figure 4.1a) (Herrlin and Belady 2006; Furihata et al. 2003) for exhaust hot-air removal. The worst ventilation scheme uses overhead chilled-air supply with exhaust vents at the floor or at the bottom part of the walls (see Figure 4.1c) (Shrivastava et al. 2005a; Nakao et al. 1991).

- The typical underfloor supply design (see Figure 4.1a) can result in hot spots at the very top part of the rack inlet due to hot-air recirculation patterns (Schmidt 2001; Sorell et al. 2005; Herrlin and Belady 2006; Furihata et al. 2003; Karlsson and Moshfegh 2003). This does not occur in overhead supply designs (see Figures 4.1b–4.1c) where chilled air is supplied from the top leading and well mixed at the top of the rack (Sorell et al. 2005, Herrlin and Belady 2006, Furihata et al. 2003).

- Of three variables, the chilled airflow supply percentage, the ceiling height, and the return hot-air vent location, the chilled airflow supply fraction had the biggest influence on rack inlet temperatures for a variety of ventilation schemes (Shrivastava et al. 2005b).

- Steep termperature gradients at the front of that rack can occur with high server density layout with underfloor chilled-air supply (Sorell et al. 2005 Schmidt and Iyengar 2007). This phenomenon is sometimes less pronounced for the same rack layout if an overhead design is employed (Sorell at al. 2005).

- Directing hot exhaust air from equipment and cabinets upward into a ceiling return plenum may be superior to simply having a high ceiling (Beaty and Davidson 2005).

- If flexibility exists in the orientation of rows of equipment, a layout that allows hot air unobstructed access to the return of CRACs (or other cooling system returns) should be superior to a layout with rows perpendicular to the CRACs. Enhancing the natural flow of the exhaust air from point A to point B should reduce the recycle potential for the warmest air (Beaty and Davidson 2005).

- Cold-aisle/hot-aisle arrangement should be followed in laying out racks within a data center; the fronts of the racks drawing in chilled air from either overhead or from the raised-access floor should face the chilled air exhausting into the cold aisle (Beaty and Davidson 2005, Beaty and Schmidt 2004, Beaty and Davidson 2003, ASHRAE 2003).

4.1.2   RAISED-ACCESS FLOOR PLENUM HEIGHT

Balancing the distribution of chilled air throughout the data processing center so that data processing units with high heat loads receive more chilled air than those with lower heat loads is a daunting task. Making a change at one location affects the airflow from all other locations. However, there are guidelines for providing the best overall airflow and modifying airflow distribution for the datacom equipment layout.

One question that arises when designing raised-access floor data centers is for what height raised-access floor should one design? Kang et al. (2001), Karki et al. (2003), Patankar and Karki (2004), and Karki and Patankar (2006) studied raised-access floors to provide an answer. The key question is what height provides the greatest flexibility for making adjustments to the airflow as datacom equipment is moved around the data center and newer datacom racks are brought in and others, possibly lower-powered racks, are moved out. The two parameters of the raised-access floor that affect the flow distribution and the ability to adjust the flow throughout the floor are the raised-access floor height and the percentage opening of the tiles on the raised-access floor. The plenum height has significant influence on the horizontal velocity and pressure distribution in the plenum. As the plenum height increases, the velocities decrease and the pressure variations diminish, leading to a more uniform airflow distribution. This can be shown analytically with the Bernoulli equation. To illustrate the effect of plenum height, Karki et al. (2003) performed an analysis on a base configuration shown in Figure 4.1a. When the raised-access floor height is not very high (6–12 in. [0.15–0.3 m]), the flow from the perforated tiles nearest the CRAC is very low, and in some cases reverse flow occurs. Thus, datacom equipment cannot be placed in this area and be adequately provided with chilled air. However, as the height of the raised-access floor increases (up to 30 in. [0.76 m]), the distribution of flow across the tiles becomes much more uniform and the reverse flow near the CRAC is eliminated. The simulations by Karki et al. (2003) were for tiles that were 25% open.

So what happens when the perforated tiles are more open, and will this allow the raised-access floor height to decrease? The variation in tile flow rates becomes much larger as one increases the perforated openings. If one desires a uniform distribution of air from perforated tiles because all the datacom equipment residing adjacent to these tiles are similar, then one can vary the perforated tile openings. Common perforated tiles typically have open free area ratios of 6%, 11%, 25%, 40%, and 60%. To make the flow distribution uniform, it is necessary to encourage the flow near the CRAC and discourage it at positions away from the CRAC.

Recommendations/Guidelines

- For low raised-access floors (6–12 in. [0.15–0.3 m]), do not place datacom equipment close to CRACs since low airflow or reverse flow can occur from the perforated tiles.
- Airflow from a large number of perforated tiles can be made uniform if perforated tiles of varying percent openings are distributed so that some areas have higher percent openings to encourage more flow, while some areas have less percent openings to discourage flow.
- Partitions can be placed underneath the raised-access floor to direct air into the desired areas.
- Modeling suggests that raised-access floors should be designed to allow a free flow height of at least 24 in. (0.61 m); if piping and cabling take up 6 in., then the raised-access floor height should be 30 in. (0.76 m) (Patankar and Karki 2004; Beaty and Davidson 2005). A large underfloor depth of 24 in. (0.61 m) was also recommended by VanGilder and Schmidt (2005).

4.1.3   ROOM CEILING HEIGHT

The ceiling height depends on the type of ventilation system that is chosen. Sorell et al. (2006) studied the effect of ceiling height on three ventilation schemes: underfloor air distribution without ceiling, underfloor air distribution with ceiling, and overhead air distribution without ceiling. The three ceiling heights investigated were 12 ft (3.7 m), 14 ft (4.3 m), and 16 ft (4.9 m). The room analyzed was approximately 10,000 ft^2 with the datacom equipment in a cold-aisle/hot-aisle arrangement and the CRACs situated around the perimeter of the room. The flow from the CRACs was set to 110% of the total datacom equipment airflow. In this study, the increased ceiling height improved the air inlet temperatures for all the ventilation schemes studied. However, Sorell et al. (2006) mentions that while their study showed increased height aided the inlet air temperatures, care must be taken not to increase the height too much since increased building costs could become a major factor. An earlier study by Schmidt (2001) for a data center with underfloor air distribution without a ceiling return showed that increasing the ceiling height from 8 to 10 ft actually increased inlet temperatures to the datacom equipment, in some cases quite dramatically. For cases where the flow exiting the perforated tiles did not match or exceed the rack flow rate, a hot recirculation cell developed at the top of the racks. This cell increased in intensity as the ceiling height increased, allowing the the datacom equipment to ingest the hot air much more readily. In addition to a comparison between model and experimental data, a parametric ceiling height study was also conducted by Shrivastava et al. (2006). Kopin (2003) discussed future data center needs in the context of existing infrastructure and also addressed the height parameter in data center design.

Recommendations/Guidelines

- When the supply chilled air from the perforated tiles exceeds the rack flow rates (110%), increasing the ceiling height reduces the datacom equipment intake temperatures for three cases: (1) underfloor chilled-air supply and room CRAC hot-air return with a hood at the top of the CRAC, (2) underfloor air supply and ceiling hot air return that vents to the CRAC, and (3) overhead air supply and room CRAC hot-air return at the bottom of the CRAC (Sorell et al. 2006).
- For flows from the perforated tiles equal to or less than the datacom equipment flow rates, increasing the ceiling height can result in increased inlet temperatures for underfloor air distribution. A hot recirculation cell intensifies over the datacom equipment with increased height (Schmidt 2001).
- Increasing the ceiling height from 9 ft (2.74 m) to 12 ft (3.65 m) reduces the rack inlet temperature by as much as 11°F–22°F (6°C–12°C) in hot spot regions and has small impact (inconsistent) in lower flux regions for 6 ft (1.8 m) tall racks arranged in a hot-aisle/cold-aisle fashion on a raised-access floor (Shrivastava et al. 2005).

- Increasing the ceiling height beyond 12 ft (3.65 m) for 6 ft (1.82 m) racks does not seem to have any impact on rack inlet temperatures for racks arranged in a hot aisle/cold aisle fashion on a raised-access floor with under-floor supply and room CRAC return (Shrivastava et al. 2005).

4.1.4   UNDERFLOOR BLOCKAGES

Placement of Underfloor Cabling, Chilled-Water Pipes, and Partitions Under Raised-Access Floor

The recommendation regarding the installation of cabling and equipment can be found in a report published by the Telecommunications Industry Association (TIA 2005).

ANSI/TIA-942 Recommendations/Guidelines

- Perforated access floor tiles should be located in the cold aisles rather than in the hot aisles to improve the functioning of hot and cold aisles.
- No cable trays or other obstruction should be placed in the cold aisles below the perforated tiles.
- Telecommunications cabling under the access floor shall be in ventilated cable trays that do not block airflow. Additional cable tray design considerations are provided in ANSI/TIA-569-B (TIA 2003).
- Underfloor cable tray routing should be coordinated with other underfloor systems during the planning stages of the building. Readers are referred to NEMA VE 2-2001 (NEMA 2001) for recommendations regarding installation of cable trays.

Detrimental Underfloor Blockages

The raised-access floor within a data center usually serves multiple functions. Not only does the raised-access floor plenum provide air distribution to the datacom equipment, it also provides a means for distributing cables that interconnect the datacom equipment. In addition, piping that provides chilled water to the CRACs is usually installed under the raised-access floor. Structural beams under the floor also create airflow blockages. Unless care is taken placing these airflow blockages, the airflow exiting perforated tiles can be dramatically affected. In addition to studies by Schmidt et al. (2004) and VanGilder and Schmidt (2005), Bhopte et al. (2006) performed parametric numerical (CFD) analyses on a raised-access floor data center and characterized the effect of underfloor blockages on the air temperature at the inlet of server racks for a typical representative floor plan.

Recommendations/Guidelines

- If possible, chilled-water pipes and cabling should be kept away from the exhaust of the CRACs (Schmidt et al. 2004).
- Underfloor blockages have the biggest influence on flow rate uniformity through the perforated tiles (VanGilder and Schmidt 2005).
- Blockages that are parallel to the hot and cold aisles have much lower impact than those that run perpendicular to the aisle lengths in cases where CRACs are located parallel to the computer rack equipment aisles (Bhopte et al. 2006).
- Blockages occurring under the cold aisle have the effect of reducing perforated tile flow rates (Bhopte et al. 2006).

Beneficial Underfloor Blockages

Karki et al. (2003) and Bhopte et al. (2006) showed that some blockages within the plenum can aid in the distribution of air exiting the raised-access floor perforated tiles. This may be desirable if more airflow is needed in an area that has higher powered datacom equipment or where one wants to better distribute the airflow, given that only one size of perforated tile is available. Karki et al. (2003) showed that selectively positioned partitions in the underfloor plenum can result in better perforated tile airflow distribution. In this case, the inclined partitions were arranged so the flows from the tiles were fairly uniform. Another variation of flow partitions was shown by Karki et al. (2003), where perforated partitions are arranged in the flow path exiting the CRAC. Bhopte et al. (2006) showed that when blockages channel flow into a cold aisle (e.g., chilled-water pipes that are on both sides of a cold aisle), there is favorable airflow distribution through the tiles.

4.1.5   CRAC PLACEMENT AND CONFIGURATION

The location and configuration of the CRACs can influence the data center cooling in many ways. Several previous studies have investigated these effects.

Recommendations/Guidelines

- If flexibility exists in the placement of the CRACs, place them facing the hot aisle rather than cold aisles, as the underfloor velocity pressure should be minimized in cold aisles (Beaty and Davidson 2005; Schmidt and Iyengar 2005).
- If CRACs are aligned in parallel rows on a raised-access floor, then each row of CRACs should exhaust air in a direction that increases the static pressure across the floor rather than a way in which their plumes collide, causing decreased static pressure in these regions and overall loss of chilled air to the raised-access floor (Koplin 2003).

- Racks that have a clear path of hot air back to the intakes of the CRACs generally show low rack air temperatures (Beaty and Davidson 2005; Schmidt and Iyengar 2005).

- Separating the cold air and hot exhaust air are key to improved energy efficiency of the ventilation system.

- For better temperature control of the air inlet to the IT equipment , the CRACs should be controlled on outlet air from the CRACs and not inlet air returning from the racks.

- Airflow rate distribution in the perforated tiles is more uniform when all the CRACs discharge in the same direction, and distribution is poor (nonuniform) when the CRACs discharge air such that the air streams collide with each other (Schmidt et al. 2004).

- Turning vanes and baffles appeared to reduce the CRAC airflow rate by about 15%. It is thus preferable that turning vanes (scoops) not be used in CRACs (Schmidt et al. 2004). However, when turning vanes are used on CRACs facing each other, their orientation should be such that the airflow from the CRACs are in the same direction (Schmidt et al. 2004).

- Integrating sophisticated thermal instrumentation and control of a data center environment with the operation parameters of CRACs (Boucher et al. 2004; Bash et al. 2006) (e.g., volumetric airflow rate or chilled-air setpoint temperature) can result in significant energy saving of around 50% (Bash et al. 2006). VFD can be used to change fan speeds and, thus, CRAC airflow rates, and the chilled-air setpoint temperatures can be changed by controlling the condenser conditions of the CRAC (Boucher et al. 2004).

4.2   ACCOMMODATING FUTURE DATA CENTER GROWTH

Kurkjian and Glass (2004) summarize the planning to accommodate the various load conditions of the mechanical systems for a recently designed data center, including raised-access floor cooling, central plants, and pipe distribution. During the design phase, the project designers are asked to plan for any of the computing equipment placed anywhere on the raised-access floor. In addition, it is desirable to accommodate technology changes and load increases that occur throughout the life of the data center. These are extremely difficult criteria that require good communication between the data center owner/operator and the designer.

Recommendations/Guidelines

- Develop phased plans for the installation of mechanical and electrical equipment, matching cooling and electrical infrastructure to IT requirements, and thereby only incurring infrastructure cost when required (Kurkjian and Glass 2004; Beaty and Schmidt 2004).

- The maximum capability of the infrastructure that will accommodate the last phase installation of datacom equipment will determine the corresponding sizes of the mechanical and electrical rooms (Kurkjian and Glass 2004).
- Place capped valves in those locations where CRACs can be installed to support future IT equipment (Kurkjian and Glass 2004).
- Capped valves can also accommodate future computing equipment technologies that require direct connection of chilled water through a heat exchanger to a secondary loop that cools the electronics. The heat transfer mediums for cooling the electronics could be water, refrigerants, fluroinerts, or other currently undetermined mediums for cooling (Kurkjian and Glass 2004; Beaty and Schmidt 2004).
- There are three advantages to placing the CRACs and piping in corridors around the perimeter of the IT equipment room (Kurkjian and Glass 2004): (1) maintenance of the CRACs is removed from the data center, (2) piping is installed in the corridor and not on the main floor so that any valves that need to be exercised are not inside the data center, and (3) future CRAC installations are limited to the corridor and do not intrude on the data center floor.
- Eliminate reheat coils and humidification from the local CRACs and incorporate those in the central AHUs (Kurkjian and Glass 2004).
- New data centers constructed completely inside the building (no common exterior wall) with vapor barriers provided on the data center walls minimize the effect of the outdoor environment (Kurkjian and Glass 2004).
- To minimize data center construction, typically all piping systems are installed to meet future design loads (Kurkjian and Glass 2004; Beaty and Schmidt 2004). Two approaches provide fault-tolerant piping systems: (1) dual chilled-water supply and return to all air conditioners, which makes completely redundant supply and return piping systems available to all equipment in the event of a failure and (2) install chilled-water supply and return piping loops around all of the CRACs where isolation valves are used that permit all equipment to be fed from either direction of the loop.

4.3   RAISED-ACCESS FLOOR DATA CENTER

4.3.1   PERFORATED TILE LAYOUT AND CONFIGURATION

Schmidt et al. (2004) presented experimental and numerical CFD data for airflow rates through perforated tiles for various tile layouts and CRAC configurations. The CRAC configurations considered by Schmidt et al. (2004) included number of units, location, and the use of turning vanes. VanGilder and Schmidt (2005) carried out numerical simulations for a large number of raised-access floor models based on actual data centers. They quantified the impact of underfloor blockages, floor plan (tile layout), plenum depth, airflow leakage rate, and total airflow rate on the flow rate uniformity through the perforated tiles. Radmehr et al. (2005)

also conducted an experimental and numerical study on raised-access floor data centers, but emphasized chilled-air leakage from the seams in the panels along the perimeter of all the tiles, both perforated and solid. Beaty (2005) provided a high level assessment of the different factors involved in commissioning a raised-access floor data center with underfloor chilled-air supply, from a practitioner's perspective. Other studies were conducted by Schmidt and Cruz (2002, 2003a), Beaty and Davidson (2005), and Schmidt and Iyengar (2005) that included the effect of chilled-air entry into the hot aisle via tiles or cable openings.

Recommendations/Guidelines

- Perforated tiles (and, thus, racks) should not be located very close to the CRACs. Tiles can draw air from the room very close to the CRACs due to localized high velocities and, therefore, low static pressures caused by the Bernoulli effect (Schmidt et al. 2004).
- Airflow rate uniformity through the perforated tiles can be achieved by using restrictive tiles (e.g., 25% open), minimizing blockages, increasing plenum depth, reducing leakage flow, and using a hot-aisle/cold-aisle configuration (VanGilder and Schmidt 2005).
- While restrictive tiles can improve tile flow uniformity, this is not recommended in hot spot areas where it is beneficial to supply as much chilled air as possible to the cold aisle.
- The hot-aisle/cold-aisle arrangement is a good design, but the rows of more than ten tiles should be avoided when there is a CRAC on one end and a wall on the other (VanGilder and Schmidt 2005).
- If the seams in the floor tiles are sealed, then distributed air leakage can be reduced by 5%–15% in a data center (Radmehr et al. 2005).
- Dampers should not be used in perforated tiles and, if present, they should be removed. The damper element can move over time, and setting the position of the damper can be problematic. It is much better to have perforated tiles with different percentages of open area to allow optimizing the ventilation of a raised-access floor.
- Unused cable openings should be closed since they allow supply air to go where it is not needed. If these openings are large or frequent enough, they also allow the static pressure to bleed from the raised-access floor plenum (Beaty and Davidson 2005).
- The more maldistributed the flow exiting the perforated tiles along a cold aisle, the lower are the average rack inlet temperatures bordering the aisle. For higher tile flows, the maldistribution did not have as large an effect at the highest-powered rack locations (Schmidt and Cruz 2003a).
- Where high-powered racks draw from multiple perforated tiles, inlet air temperatures can be maintained within temperature specifications (Schmidt and Iyengar 2005).

- If the hot aisle is too hot for servicing, then a limited number of perforated tiles can be placed in the hot aisle to encourage thermal dilution (Beaty and Davidson 2005; Schmidt and Iyengar 2005).
- Inlet air temperatures increased as more chilled air shifted to the hot aisle. The most efficient use of the chilled air is to exhaust it in the cold aisle such that it washes the fronts of the racks (Schmidt and Cruz 2002a).

4.3.2   RACK AND RACK LAYOUT-RELATED EFFECTS

There are several rack-related data center design variables that can significantly influence the thermal environment. These factors may include rack placement, rack airflow rates, magnitude of rack heat loads (whether uniform or nonuniform), hot-aisle/cold-aisle spacing, partitions, and localized cooling using refrigeration or liquid-cooled heat exchangers.

Effect of Rack Placement

Recommendations/Guidelines

- Placement of high density datacom equipment at floor locations that have high static pressure allows the highest possible airflow in the cold aisle adjacent to the equipment (Beaty and Davidson 2005). Typically, the highest static pressures are further away from the CRACs or where the flows from two or more CRACs are in collision with each other.
- The recirculation of hot air can be reduced by load spreading. By placing lower-powered equipment near high-powered equipment, the effect of hot-air recirculation can be reduced (Beaty and Davidson 2005).
- Flow near the end of an aisle should be considered in detail, as recirculation can occur both around the sides and over the top of the cabinet (Schmidt 2001; Beaty and Davidson 2005; Rambo and Joshi 2003a, 2003b). Some data centers employ plastic stripes at the end of an aisle to prevent air recirculation but allow ease of access.
- If server inlet temperatures, as measured by ASHRAE thermal guidelines (ASHRAE 2003), are much less than that required by the manufacturer, then reducing airflow by turning off or reducing air conditioning can result in significant energy savings (Schmidt et al. 2006).
- The inlet air temperature to high-powered racks can be reduced significantly by removing an adjacent rack (Schmidt and Cruz 2003c). Racks in the vicinity of the removed racks also experience a reduced inlet air temperature.
- Schmidt and Cruz (2002b) found that for some layouts, the best position for high-powered racks is near the end of the aisles. However, more recent studies found the outside racks at the ends of the aisles can experience more hot-air recirculation (Schmidt and Iyengar 2007).

Effect of Rack Flows and Rack/Heat Loads

Recommendations/Guidelines

- In order to maintain a given inlet temperature, the chilled airflow rate exhausting from the perforated tiles should increase with increased rack flow rate (Schmidt and Cruz 2003b).
- Decreasing rack flow rates increased rack air inlet temperatures. Higher rack flow tends to increase the mixing in the data center, thereby lowering the air that is drawn into the racks (Schmidt and Cruz 2003b).
- Conditions necessary and sufficient to meet rack inlet temperatures for high-powered racks (>10 kW) with moderate (18°F–36°F [10°C–20°C]) rack air temperature rise: (1) perforated tiles immediately in front a rack must supply one-quarter to one-half of the rack flow rate and another ~25% supply from the cable cutout openings (Schmidt 2004; Schmidt et al. 2005a, 2006), and (2) CRAC capability in the region of the racks must be equal to or greater in capacity to handle localized hot spot rack heat load (Schmidt 2004; Schmidt et al. 2005a, 2006).
- For data centers with low-powered racks (1–3 kW/rack), for fully populated racks, a chilled-air supply of 50% is sufficient to meet inlet air temperatures (Furihata et al. 2004a).
- When the rack air temperature rise is greater than 36°F (20°C) for high-powered racks (>10 kW), it is anticipated that closer to 100% chiller air supply fraction will be needed.
- To eliminate the recirculation of hot air from the rear of a rack over the top of the rack and into the front of the rack near the top, the front cover can be designed to restrict air draw into the rack to only the bottom portions of the rack (Wang 2004).
- The IT industry provides guidelines for airflow within a rack: front to back, front to top, and front to back and top (Beaty and Davidson 2003; ASHRAE 2004).

Effect of Aisle Spacing

The most common aisle spacings are 4 ft aisles, which are consistent with two floor tiles for the hot aisle and cold aisle. With the increased server rack powers, Beaty and Davidson (2005) suggest the aisle widths be increased to allow for more air in the vicinity of the IT equipment at a possibly reduced velocity. Limiting the velocity of the air supply by the perforated tiles has two benefits: high-velocity air tends to blow by the inlet grilles of the servers, and high-velocity air near the center of the aisle tends to blow by the intake of the servers and out the top of the aisle without benefit to cooling.

Recommendations/Guidelines

- Wider cold aisles increase chilled air to the servers and lower the velocity exiting the tiles, thereby eliminating a potential blow by of high-velocity chilled air (Beaty and Davidson 2005).

Partitions at the End of Aisles, Above Racks, Within Racks, and Between Racks

Recommendations/Guidelines

- Strategically placed ceiling partitions may help prevent recirculation of hot exhaust air into the inlets of the servers, but consideration of placement of these partitions must take into account local fire codes (Beaty and Davidson 2005).
- To prevent recirculation within a rack, it is important to install blanking panels for those areas of the rack without servers installed and also in those areas where there is a clear path for hot air from the rear to the front of the servers (Beaty and Davidson 2005). Gap partitioning between the different units in a rack helps reduce rack inlet temperature (Furihata et al. 2004a).
- Gaps between low-powered racks may be acceptable since little airflow is needed for low-powered racks and most, if not all, of the air can come from the perforated tiles (Schmidt and Iyengar 2005).
- Gaps between high-powered racks arranged in a hot-aisle/cold-aisle fashion should be eliminated. They can cause significant infiltration of hot exhaust air from the racks directly into the neighboring cold aisles (Schmidt et al. 2006). This can lead to rack inlet temperatures higher by as much as 11°F (6°C) (Schmidt et al. 2006).
- For data centers with lower-powered racks (1.5 kW/rack), the facility air-conditioning efficiency can be improved by about 5% by restricting the rack air intake opening to the bottom one-third portion of the front of the rack (Furihata et al. 2003; 2004b). Thus, the location of the intake and exit openings can influence energy efficiency.
- For data centers with lower powered racks (1–3 kW/rack), using fully populated racks results in less hot exhaust air recirculation than using partially filled racks (Furihata et al. 2004a).

4.4   LOCALIZED COOLING

Patel et al. (2001) displays measurements and modeling of a prototype data center whereby heat exchangers installed over the datacom racks is used to extract heat from the racks and cold air is exhausted from the heat exchangers into the cold aisles. Schmidt et al. (2005b) demonstrated the use of a water-cooled heat exchanger that was integrated into the rear door of the server racks. Leonard (2005) describes a thermal bus concept in which passive loop thermosiphons are used to transfer the computer server processor heat load to a rack-level location for rejection to facility-chilled water.

Recommendations/Guidelines

- Placing the cooling near the source of heat shortens the distance the air must be moved. This increases the capacity, flexibility, efficiency, and scalability of the cooling systems (Baer 2004; Schmidt et al. 2005b; Heydari and Sabounchi 2004).
- Placing liquid-cooling units at the end of rows can eliminate or reduce the wrap around effect of hot air from the rear of racks.
- Localized rack cooling can more closely match the rack power load and thereby greatly improve the overall data center efficiency.

4.5   NON-RAISED-ACCESS FLOOR DATA CENTER

Sorell at el. (2005), Iyengar et al. (2005), and Schmidt and Iyengar (2007) used CFD modeling to characterize and study non-raised-access floor data centers. While Sorell et al. (2005) and Schmidt and Iyengar (2007) compared non-raised-access and raised-access floor designs, Iyengar et al. (2005) investigated the effect of several parameters unique to non-raised-access floor designs, such as diffuser angle and the height of diffuser location.

Recommendations/Guidelines

- Use ~30° diffusers if you want to reduce the temperatures at the top of the racks, and do not use diffusers (blowing air straight down) if the temperatures at the bottom of the racks need to be cool (Iyengar et al. 2005).
- Using the air supply diffuser close to the top of the racks helps the bottom of the racks, and a larger clearance helps the tops of the racks (Iyengar et al. 2005).
- High rack heat loads can mean high rack flow rates and better mixing; this can sometimes reduce the inlet air temperature to the rack (Iyengar et al. 2005).
- The air at the top of the rack is usually hotter than at the bottom, even though this effect is not as pronounced as underfloor air supply designs (Sorell et al. 2005; Iyengar et al. 2005).

4.6   DATA CENTER ENERGY MANAGEMENT AND EFFICIENCY

As rack heat loads increase, leading to a rise in cluster power consumption, energy management and efficiency of the cooling design plays a key role in the design of data centers from a total cost of ownership (TCO) perspective. Significant energy savings were demonstrated by the use of the localized cooling described in an earlier section, which employs liquid-based cooling techniques to augment more traditional CRAC-driven air cooling (Patel et al. 2001; Schmidt et al. 2005b; Leonard et al. 2005). Patel et al. (2003) present a smart cooling holistic methodology for data center thermal management on a global level by combining localized cooling with server workload allocation to allow the data center to function at its most energy efficient. Patel et al. (2002) studied the impact of nonuniformity in rack heat load distribution on the energy efficiency of the air-cooling units with an emphasis on CRAC load balancing, rack and CRAC layout optimization, and CRAC sizing. White and Abels (2004) discuss energy management via software-based algorithms in a dynamic virtual data center. Herold and Rademacher (2002) described a natural gas turbine power driven data center that incorporates waste heat recovery using absorption (ASHRAE 2006) chillers. CRAC thermal parameter control proposed by Boucher et al. (2004) and Bash et al. (2006) are discussed in a preceding CRAC configuration section.

More recently, a comprehensive design guide provided by the Pacific Gas and Electric Company (PG&E 2006) and developed by Rumsey Engineers and researchers at LBNL in California, resulted in a set of guidelines for energy efficient data center design. Some of these best practices are listed below:

- Using centralized air handlers means using larger size, more efficient fans.
- Optimize a refrigeration plant using higher building chiller water temperature setpoints, variable flow evaporators and staging controls, lower condenserwater temperature setpoints, high-efficiency VFDs in chiller pumps, and thermal storage units to handle peak loads.
- Water-cooled chillers can offer significant energy savings over air-cooled chillers, particularly in dry climates. Among the options of water-cooled chillers, variable-speed centrifugal are the most energy efficient.
- Variable-speed fans on cooling towers allow for optimized tower control.
- Premium efficiency motors and high-efficiency pumps are recommended.
- Localize liquid cooling of racks to augment air-handling capabilities of existing cooling infrastructure.
- Use of free cooling via a water-side economizer to cool building chilled water in mild outdoor conditions and bypass the refrigeration system.
- Humidity control is very energy intensive. It is also difficult to sustain due to susceptibility to sensor drift. Waste heat in the return airstream can be used for adiabatic humidification. A common control signal can be used to ensure all CRACs are set to the same humidity setpoint.
- Use high-reliability generation units as the primary power source with the grid as back up; also use waste-heat recovery systems, such as adsorption chillers. This allows the elimination of backup power sources.
- Use high-efficiency UPS systems. For battery-based power backup, use as high a load factor as possible, with at least 40% or higher of their rated capacity. This may require the use of smaller battery-operated UPS systems in parallel.
- Use power conditioning to operate the system in the most line-efficient mode for line-reactive systems.

ASHRAE recently published a book as part of the Datacom Series titled *Best Practices for Datacom Facility Energy Efficiency* (ASHRAE 2008). This book contains a number of additional recommendations related to energy efficiency, and the reader is encouraged to consult it for further details.

5

References and Bibliography

Anton, R., H. Jonsson, and B. Palm. 2002. Modeling of air conditioning systems for cooling of data centers. *Proceedings of the Intersociety Conference on Thermal Phenomena (ITherm), San Diego, CA,* pp. 552–58.

ASHRAE. 2004. *Thermal Guidelines for Data Centers and Other Data Processing Environments.* Atlanta: American Society of Heating, Refrigerating and Air-Conditioning Engineers, Inc.

ASHRAE. 2005. *Guideline 0-2005, The Commissioning Process.* Atlanta: American Society of Heating, Refrigerating and Air-Conditioning Engineers, Inc.

ASHRAE. 2005. *Datacom Equipment Power Trends and Cooling Applications.* Atlanta: American Society of Heating, Refrigerating and Air-Conditioning Engineers, Inc.

ASHRAE. 2006. *2006 ASHRAE Handbook—Refrigeration.* Atlanta: American Society of Heating, Refrigerating and Air-Conditioning Engineers, Inc.

Baer, D. 2004. Managing data center heat density. *HPAC Engineering* February:44–7.

Bash, C.B. 2000. A hybrid approach to plate fin-tube heat exchanger analysis. *Proceedings of the International Conference and Exhibition on High Density Interconnect and Systems Packaging, Denver, Colorado,* pp. 40–8.

Bash, C., C. Patel, and R. Sharma. 2006. Dynamic thermal management of air cooled data centers. *Proceedings of the Intersociety Conference on Thermal Phenomena (ITherm), San Diego, CA.*

Beaty, D. 2005. Cooling data centers with raised-floor plenums, heating piping air conditioning. *HPAC Engineering* 77(9):58–65.

Beaty, D., and R. Schmidt. 2004. Back to the future: Liquid cooling data center considerations. *ASHRAE Journal* 46(12):42–6.

Beaty, D., and T. Davidson. 2003. New guideline for data center cooling. *ASHRAE Journal* 45(12):28–34.

Beaty, D., and T. Davidson. 2005. Data centers—Datacom airflow patterns. *ASHRAE Journal* 47(4):50–54.

Beaty, D., N. Chauhan, and D. Dyer. 2005a. High density cooling of data centers and telecom facilities—Part 1. *ASHRAE Transactions* 111(1):921–31.

Beaty, D., N. Chauhan, and D. Dyer. 2005b. High Density Cooling of Data Centers and Telecom Facilities—Part 2. *ASHRAE Transactions* (111)1:932–44.

Bedekar, V., S. Karajgikar, D. Agonafer, M. Iyengar, and R. Schmidt. 2006. Effect of CRAC location on fixed rack layout. *Proceedings of the Intersociety Conference on Thermal Phenomena (ITherm), San Diego, CA.*

Belady, C., and C. Malone. 2006. Data center power projections to 2014. *Proceedings of the Intersociety Conference on Thermal Phenomena (ITherm), San Diego, CA.*

Belady, C., and D. Beaty. 2005. Data centers—Roadmap for datacom cooling. *ASHRAE Journal* 47(12):52–5.

Bhopte, S., R. Schmidt, D. Agonafer, and B. Sammakia. 2005. Optimization of data center room layout to minimize rack inlet air temperature. *Proceedings of Interpack, San Francisco, CA.*

Bhopte, S., B. Sammakia, R. Schmidt, M. Iyengar, and D. Agonafer. 2006. Effect of under floor blockages on data center performance. *Proceedings of the Intersociety Conference on Thermal Phenomena (ITherm), San Diego, CA.*

Boucher, T., D. Auslander, C. Bash, C. Federspiel, and C. Patel. 2004. Viability of dynamic cooling control in a data center environment. *Proceedings of the Intersociety Conference on Thermal Phenomena (ITherm), Las Vegas, NV,* pp. 593–600.

ERA. 2003. European workplace noise directive. Directive 2003/10/EC, European Rotogravure Association, Munich, Germany.

Flometrics. 1999. Flovent version 2.1. Flometrics Ltd., Surrey, England.

Furihata, Y., H. Hayama, M. Enai, and T. Mori. 2003. Efficient cooling system for it equipment in a data center. *Proceedings of the International Telecommunications Energy Conference (INTELEC), Yokohama, Japan,* pp. 152–59.

Furihata, Y., H. Hayama, M. Enai, and T. Mori, and M. Kishita. 2004a. Improving the efficiency of cooling systems in data centers considering equipment characteristics. *Proceedings of the International Telecommunications Energy Conference (INTELEC), Chicago, IL,* pp. 32–37.

Furihata, Y., H. Hayama, M. Enai, and T. Mori. 2004b. The effect of air intake format of equipment gives to air conditioning systems in a data center. *IEICE Transactions on Communications* 87(12):3568–75.

Guggari, S., D. Agonafer, C. Belady, and L. Stahl. 2003. A hybrid methodology for the optimization of data center room layout. *Proceedings of the Pacific Rim/ASME International Electronics Packaging Technical Conference and Exhibition (InterPack), Maui, Hawaii.*

Hamann, H., J. Lacey, M. O'Boyle, R. Schmidt, and M. Iyengar. 2005. Rapid 3-dimensional thermal characterization of large scale computing facilities.

International Microelectronics and Packaging Society (IMAPS) Sympo-sium—Advanced Thermal Workshop, October.

Hayama, H., M. Enai, T. Mori, and M. Kishita. 2003. Planning of air conditioning and circulation systems for data center. *Proceedings of the International Tele-communications Energy Conference (INTELEC), Yokohama, Japan*, pp. 152–59.

Hayama, H., M. Enai, T. Mori, and M. Kishita. 2004. Planning of air conditioning and circulation systems for data center. *IEICE Transactions on Communica-tions* 87(12):3443–50.

Herold, K., and R. Rademacher. 2002. Integrated power and cooling systems for data centers. *Proceedings of the Intersociety Conference on Thermal Phenom-ena (ITherm), San Diego, CA*, pp. 808–11.

Herrlin, M. 2005. Rack cooling effectiveness in data centers and telecom central offices: The rack cooling index (RCI). *ASHRAE Transactions* 111(2):725–31.

Herrlin, M., and C. Belady. 2006. Gravity assisted air mixing in data centers and how it affects the rack cooling effectiveness. *Proceedings of the Intersociety Conference on Thermal Phenomena (ITherm), San Diego, CA.*

Heydari, A., and P. Sabounchi. 2004. Refrigeration assisted spot cooling of a high heat density data center. *Proceedings of the Intersociety Conference on Ther-mal Phenomena (ITherm), Las Vegas, NV,* pp. 601–06.

IEC. 2005. Electromagnetic compatibility (EMC)—Part 3-2: Limits—Limits for harmonic current emissions (equipment input current ≤16A per phase). Inter-national Electrotechnical Commission, Geneva, Switzerland.

Iyengar, M., R. Schmidt, A. Sharma, G. McVicker, S. Shrivastava, S. Sri-Jayantha, Y. Anemiya, H. Dang, T. Chainer, and B. Sammakia. 2005. Thermal charac-terization of non-raised floor air cooled data centers using numerical model-ing. *Proceedings of Interpack, San Francisco, CA.*

Kang, S., R. Schmidt, K. Kelkar, A. Radmehr, and S. Patankar. 2001. A methodol-ogy for the design of perforated tiles in raised floor data centers using compu-tational flow analysis. *IEEE Transactions on Components and Packaging Technologies* 24(2):177–83.

Karki, K., and S. Patankar. 2006. Air flow distribution through perforated tiles in raised floor data centers. *Transactions of Buildings and Environment* 41(6):734–44.

Karki, K., S. Patankar, and A. Radmehr. 2003. Techniques for controlling airflow distribution in raised floor data centers. *Proceedings of Interpack, Maui, Hawaii.*

Karlsson, J.F., and B. Moshfegh. 2003. Investigation of indoor climate and power usage in a data center. *Transactions of Energy and Buildings* 37(10):1075–83.

Koplin, E.C. 2003. Data center cooling. *ASHRAE Journal* 45(3):46–53.

Kurkjian, C., and J. Glass. 2004. Air-conditioning design for data centers accom-modating current loads and planning for the future. *ASHRAE Transactions* 111(2):715–24.

Leonard, P. 2005. Thermal bus opportunity—A quantum leap in data center cooling potential. *ASHRAE Transactions* 111(2):732–45.

Meuer, H. 2008. Top 500 supercomputer sites. http://www.top500.org/.

Nakao, M., H. Hayama, and M. Nishioka. 1991. Which cooling air supply system is better for a high heat density room: Underfloor or overhead. *Proceedings of the International Telecommunications Energy Conference (INTELEC), Kyoto, Japan,* pp. 393–400.

NEMA. 2001. Recommended practice for installing metal cable tray systems. Report VE 2-2001, National Electrical Manufacturers Associations, Rosslyn, VA.

Noh, H., K. Song, and S.K. Chun. 1998. The cooling characteristic on the air supply and return flow system in the telecommunication cabinet room. *Proceedings of the International Telecommunications Energy Conference (INTELEC), San Francisco, CA,* pp. 777–84.

Norota, M., H. Hayama, M. Enai, and M. Kishita. 2003. Research on efficiency of air conditioning system for data center. *Proceedings of International Telecommunications Energy Conference (INTELEC), Yokohama, Japan,* pp. 147–51.

PG&E. 2006. High performance data centers—A design guidelines sourcebook. Report developed by Rumsey Engineers and Lawrence Berkeley National Laboratory for the Pacific Gas and Electric Company, San Francisco, CA.

Patel, C., C. Bash, and C. Belady. 2001. Computational fluid dynamics modeling of high compute density data centers to assure system inlet air specifications. *Proceedings of InterPACK 2001 Conference, Kauai, Hawaii.*

Patel, C., R. Sharma, C. Bash, and A. Beitelmal. 2002. Thermal consideratons in cooling large scale high compute density data centers. *Proceedings of the Intersociety Conference on Thermal Phenomena (ITherm), San Diego, CA.*

Patel, C., C. Bash, R. Sharma, M. Beitelmal, and R. Friedrich. 2003. Smart cooling of data centers. *Proceedings of Interpack, Maui, Hawaii.*

Patankar, S.V., and K.C. Karki. 2004. Distribution of cooling airflow in a raised flow data center. *ASHRAE Transactions* :629-634.

Patterson, M., R. Steinbrecher, and S. Montgomery. 2005. Data centers: Comparing data center and computer thermal design. *ASHRAE Journal* :38–42.

Radmehr, A., R. Schmidt, K. Karki, and S. Patankar. 2005. Distributed leakage flow in raised floor data centers. *Proceedings of Interpack, San Francisco, CA.*

Rambo, J., and Y. Joshi. 2003a. Multi-scale modeling of high power density data centers. *Proceedings of Interpack, Maui, Hawaii.*

Rambo, J., and Y. Joshi. 2003b. Physical models in data center air flow simulations. *Proceedings of the ASME International Mechanical Engineering Exposition and Congress (IMECE), Washington, DC.*

Rambo, J., and Y. Joshi. 2005. Reduced order modeling of steady turbulent flows using the POD. *Proceedings of the ASME Summer Heat Transfer Conference, San Francisco, CA.*

Richardson, G. 2001. Traversing for accuracy in a rectangular duct. *Associated Air Balance Council Tab Journal* Summer 2001:20–27.

Schmidt, R. 2001 Effect of data center characteristics on data processing equipment inlet temperatures. *Proceedings of Interpack, Kauai, Hawaii.*

Schmidt, R. 2004. Thermal profile of a high density data center—Methodology to thermally characterize a data center. *ASHRAE Transactions* 110(2):

Schmidt, R., and E. Cruz. 2002a. Raised floor computer data center: Effect on rack inlet temperatures of chilled air exiting both the hot and cold aisles. *Proceedings of the Intersociety Conference on Thermal Phenomena (ITherm), San Diego, CA,* pp. 580–94.

Schmidt, R., and E. Cruz. 2002b. Raised floor data center: Effect on rack inlet temperatures when high powered racks are situated amongst lower powered racks. *Proceedings of the ASME Annual Winter Meeting Conference (IMECE).*

Schmidt, R., and E. Cruz. 2003a. Cluster of high powered racks within a raised floor computer data center: Effect of perforated tile flow distribution on rack inlet temperatures. *Proceedings of the ASME International Mechanical Engineering Exposition and Congress (IMECE).*

Schmidt, R., and E. Cruz. 2003b. Raised floor computer data center: Effect of rack inlet temperatures when rack flow rates are reduced. *Proceedings of Interpack.*

Schmidt, R., and E. Cruz. 2003c. Raised floor computer data center: Effect on rack inlet temperatures when adjacent racks are removed. *Proceedings of Interpack, Maui, Hawaii.*

Schmidt, R., and H. Shaukatullah. 2003. Computer and telecommunications equipment room cooling: A review of literature. *IEEE Transactions on Components and Packaging Technologies* 26(1):89–98.

Schmidt, R., and M. Iyengar. 2005a. Effect of data center layout on rack inlet air temperatures. *Proceedings of Interpack, San Francisco, CA.*

Schmidt, R.R., and M. Iyengar. 2005b. Thermal profile of a high density data center. *ASHRAE Transactions* 111(2):765–77.

Schmidt, R., and M. Iyengar. 2007. Best practices for data center thermal management—Review of literature. *ASHRAE Transactions* 113(1):206–214.

Schmidt, R., and M. Iyengar. 2007. Comparison between under floor supply and overhead supply data center ventilation designs for high density clusters. *ASHRAE Transactions* 113(1):115–25.

Schmidt, R., K. Karki, and S. Patankar. 2004. Raised floor data center: Perforated tile flow rates for various tile layouts. *Proceedings of the Intersociety Conference on Thermal Phenomena (ITherm), Las Vegas, NV,* pp. 571–75.

Schmidt, R., M. Iyengar, and R. Chu. 2005a. Data centers—Meeting data center temperature requirements. *ASHRAE Journal* 47(4):44–8.

Schmidt, R., R. Chu, M. Ellsworth, M. Iyengar, D. Porter, V. Kamath, and B. Lehman. 2005b. Maintaining datacom rack inlet air temperatures with water cooled heat exchanger. *Proceedings of Interpack, San Francisco, CA.*

Schmidt, R., M. Iyengar, D. Beaty, and S. Shrivastava. 2005c. Thermal profile of a high density data center—Hot spot heat fluxes of 512 Watts/ft². *ASHRAE Transactions* 110(2):635–42.

Schmidt, R., E. Cruz, and M. Iyengar. 2005d. Challenges of data center thermal management. *IBM Journal of Research and Development* 49(4/5):

Schmidt, R., M. Iyengar, and S. Mayhugh. 2006. Thermal profile of world's 3rd fastest supercomputer—IBM's ASC Purple cluster. *ASHRAE Transactions* 12(2):209–19.

Server System Infrastructure (SSI) Initiative, http://ssiforum.org/default.aspx

Shah, A., V. Carey, C. Bash, and C. Patel. 2005a. Exergy based optimization strategies for multi-component data center thermal management: Part I, analysis. *Proceedings of Interpack, San Francisco, CA.*

Shah, A., V. Carey, C. Bash, and C. Patel. 2005b. Exergy based optimization strategies for multi-component data center thermal management: Part II, application and validation. *Proceedings of Interpack, San Francisco, CA.*

Sharma, R., C. Bash, and C. Patel. 2002. Dimensionless parameters for evaluation of thermal design and performance of large scale data centers. *Proceedings of the 2002 AIAA Conference, St. Lois, MO.*

Sharma, R., C. Bash, C. Patel, and M. Beitelmal. 2004. Experimental investigation of design and performance of data centers. *Proceedings of the Intersociety Conference on Thermal Phenomena (ITherm), Las Vegas, NV,* pp. 579–85.

Shrivastava, S., and J. VanGilder. 2006. A statistical prediction of cold aisle end airflow boundary conditions. *Proceedings of the Intersociety Conference on Thermal Phenomena (ITherm), San Diego, CA.*

Shrivastava, S., B. Sammakia, R. Schmidt, and M. Iyengar. 2005a. Comparative analysis of different data center airflow management configurations. *Proceedings of Interpack, San Francisco, CA.*

Shrivastava, S., B. Sammakia, M. Iyengar, and R. Schmidt. 2005b. Significance levels of factors for different airflow management configurations of data centers. *Proceedings of ASME Winter Annual Meeting (IMECE).*

Shrivastava, S., M. Iyengar, B. Sammakia, R. Schmidt, and J. VanGilder. 2006. Experimental-numerical comparison for a high-density data center: Hot spot heat fluxes in excess of 500 W/ft². *Proceedings of the Inter Society Conference on Thermal Phenomena (ITherm), San Diego, CA.*

Sorell, V., S. Escalante, and J. Yang. 2005. Comparison of overhead and underfloor air delivery systems in a data center environment using CFD Modeling, *ASHRAE Transactions* 111(2):756–64.

Sorell, V., Y. Abrogable, K. Khankari, V. Gandhi, and A. Watve. 2006. An analysis of the effects of ceiling height on air distribution in data centers. *ASHRAE Transactions* 112(1):623–31.

Stahl, L. 1993. Switch room cooling—A system concept with switch room located cooling equipment. *Proceedings of INTELEC 1993, Paris, France.*

Stahl, L., and H. Zirath. 1992. TELECOOL, A new generation of cooling systems for switching equipment. *Ericsson Review* 4:124–92.

Spinazzola, R.S. 2003. High delta T cooling server rack increases energy efficiency, reliability for data centers. *Energy Engineering* 100(2):6–21.

Tate Access Floors. 2004. Controlling air leakage from raised access floor cavities. Technical Bulletin #216, Tate Access Floors, Inc., Jessup, MD.

TIA. 2003. *ANSI/TIA-569-B, Commercial Building Standard for Telecommunications Pathways and Spaces.* Arlington, VA: Telecommunications Industry Association.

TIA. 2005. *ANSI/TIA-942, Telecommunications Infrastructure Standard for Data Centers.* Arlington, VA: Telecommunications Industry Association.

VanGilder, J.W. 2007. Capture index: An airflow-based rack cooling performance metric. *ASHARE Transactions* 113(1):126–36.

VanGilder, J., and R. Schmidt. 2005. Airflow uniformity through perforated tiles in a raised floor data center. *Proceedings of Interpack, San Francisco, CA.*

VanGilder, J., and T. Lee. 2003. A Hybrid flow network-CFD method for achieving any desired flow partitioning through floor tiles of a raised floor data centers. *Proceedings of InterPack, Maui, Hawaii.*

Wang, D. 2004. A passive solution to a difficult data center environmental problem. *Proceedings of the Inter Society Conference on Thermal Phenomena (ITherm), Las Vegas, NV,* pp. 586–92.

White, R., and T. Abels. 2004. Energy resource management in the virtual data center. *Proceedings of the IEEE Symposium on Electronics and the Environment, Scottsdale, AZ,* pp. 112–16.

6

Abbreviations and Acronyms

AC	alternating current
AHU	air-handling unit
ARI	Air-Conditioning and Refrigeration Institute
ASC	advanced simulation and computing
BMS	building management system
CDU	cooling distribution unit
CFD	computational fluid dynamics
cfm	cubic feet per minute
CRAC	computer room air-conditioning unit
CRAH	computer room air-handling unit
EDP	emergency distribution panel
EER	energy efficiency ratio
EMCS	energy management control system
FCU	fan coil unit
LBNL	Lawrence Berkeley National Laboratory
NCEP	National Center for Environmental Prediction
PDU	power distribution unit
RC	rack cooling unit
RDHX	rear door heat exchanger
RH	relative humidity
RPP	remote power panels
SAN	storage area network
SDSC	San Diego Supercomputer Center
UPS	uninterruptable power supply
VA	volt-amps

VAC	volts of alternating current
VFD	variable frequency drive
VSD	variable speed drive
w.c.	water column
wg	water gauge

Index